To: Amanda
a Beacon of Light;
Beacon of Light;
May your light
serve you well
in your awakening.
Much Love,
Corri

# EMPATHS ON THEIR SOUL PATH

A Guide to Empath Empowerment

in Your Awakening

## Corri Milner, CPC

Published June 2017

Milner, Corri
Empaths On Their Soul Path

Printed in the United States of America

Body, Mind & Spirit-General  OCC000000

ISBN 13: 978-0-69288480-5   Paperback
ISBN 10: 0-692-88480-7

First Printing, June 2017

# TABLE OF CONTENTS

# PREFACE

For those empaths yet to find their way and thrive, this book is for you. For those already finding their way, looking for additional tools, validation, and reminders, this is for you. For those seeking inspiration, this is for you. For love partners, family, and friends that want to understand the empaths in their life, this is for you.

It was a long road, 25 years to find the internal and external tools I needed to become an empowered empath. There was no information available when I began my journey, nor did I know the word empath. I didn't understand why my emotions drastically changed in a moment, for no an apparent reason. I was calm and happy in one moment, then suddenly felt stress and anxiety, followed by drain and overwhelm. I was like a leaf in the wind. Sound familiar? One may think they are going crazy. Or, it could be you're an empath. Though we have different empath experiences and gifts, we all have much in common.

I found and applied tools I needed to become an empowered empath, though it was only in 2010 after I started coaching school to become a certified professional coach, that I first heard the word "empath." It was exciting to learn for the first time who my tribe really is.

For many years I tried to quash the intuitive empath in me, to keep it hidden from others for fear of a backlash and of being judged. It was when I stopped being in judgment of myself, that I was able to embrace the value of my empath gifts. My self-acceptance along with my empath gifts, caused me to be hired as a life coach by leaders in various corporate industries and other industries, as well those with the following backgrounds: chief executive officers, senior directors, lawyers, military intelligence, finance officers, therapists, doctors, life coaches and other business owners, educators, those in healing modalities, facility management, entertainment, the arts, stay-at-home moms, and everyone in-between. To my surprise everyone I coached said they were drawn to my intuitive and empathic focus. Who knew?

I offered my clients, empaths and non-empaths, both traditional and intuitive coaching. And offered my empath clients training on the Empath Toolbox and exploring gifts they were unaware they had (all found in this book). These things profoundly shifted their lives in ways they never imagined possible.

I decided to extend my reach to more empaths, in the hope they could experience a smoother passage with these tools in their journey to self, in much less time than it took me to develop them on my own. I began an 8-12 week Empath Group Program, customized to its members on empath topics. Those that joined these Programs progressed so well that I then began my closed Facebook empath group: EMPATHS ON THEIR SOUL PATH.

In my Facebook group I've offered singular Empath Calls on various topics, with presentation and interaction (online, phone, U.S., international). Those that participated found them to rewarding and of high energy. Many empaths when first joining our group had felt worn out, confused, seeking answers and support. In a short time, people have found a new understanding of who they are, their voice, and how much we all have in common. Most in my Facebook group are empaths, some lightworkers who enjoy the inspiration and camaraderie, and some parents and partners of empaths who want to understand them.

For several years many empaths have asked me to write a book. Voila. My new online radio show of the same name, Empaths On Their Soul Path, begins soon on online radio, where we will share all things empath, including: empath professions, empath families, empath challenges, empath successes, and possibilities that propel us all forward in this exciting time we are living in.

Perhaps you will join me and the many likeminded empaths coming together from around the world, sharing in the Awakening.

Much Love,
Corri Milner


Certified Professional Coach (phone, online, U.S., int'l)
Certified Master Practitioner in Energy Leadership
Healing Meditation Trainer / Energy Reader
www.corricoaching.com

## INTRODUCTION

### Are You An Empath? Is It A Gift? A Curse? Or Both?

Questions I frequently receive:

- How do I stop absorbing negative energy?
  How do I stop absorbing other people's emotions?
- How do I know what are my emotions and physical symptoms or someone else's?
- How do I stop the overwhelming drain of being an empath?
- How do I raise my energetic frequency?
- How do I live in my own energy?

### What is an Empath?

An empath is a clairsentient first and foremost. An empath is someone who experiences others' energies in a magnified way, in sense, emotion, and sometimes physical symptoms. These energies and emotions merge and absorb into our own energy and emotions.

Until one has tools to navigate energy and to stop absorbing emotions and body symptoms of others, it is hard to decipher what belongs to you. One may feel bombarded with too much external input flooding their energy field. It's like an invasion of one's being, no different than if someone trespassed and invaded your home. Except the home that is being invaded on a regular basis, is you.

Many empaths have experienced several years of feeling unheard, ignored, and marginalized by family and others, with comments like:

- You're too sensitive
- You're too funny
- You're a know-it-all
- You're scary
- You're strange
- You're crazy

Actually ... you're GIFTED!

**Too Sensitive**

Have you heard your whole life that you're "too sensitive." You're not too anything. You are a Sensitive. It's one of your superpowers, part of your greatness. A number of people are awakening to realize this is who they are. Empathy is a character trait some people seek to develop. But being an empath is not a character trait. It is not something you develop or try on. It is who you are, how you were born to be.

**If you are absorbing others in sense, emotion, and sometimes physical symptoms, you are an empath.**

Absorbing others' energies that merges with your own is not done at will, it just happens. This book has tools to help you to the other side of frustration. You will learn tools to live in your own energy and have others' energies become peripheral like background

noise. If you are experiencing the curse of being an empath, instead of your gifts, there is much you can do.

Many empaths are drained by such things as: exhaustion, isolation, depression, mental health diagnoses, involvement with narcissists, and early childhood challenges one may have been born into. It's my hope this book will help support and light your way, that you may get to know yourself as the amazing person you are, the wonder of your gifts, and come to love your life.

Empaths are endowed with a skill set all their own, extrasensory tuning ten-fold to most, in varying ways. Extrasensory tuning is part of the empath experience. Most children are born with extrasensory tuning, i.e., extra abilities in feeling, knowingness, seeing, and hearing, but when socialized it is greatly diminished or unavailable to them. People may have some psychic abilities as they come into awareness. Empaths, however, are in their own category in the complexity of their experience, and their extrasensory tuning does not diminish when socialized.

You can try to shut down being an empath as some do, but that would metaphorically be like cutting off an arm or a leg. It is how you feel the world and the lens you see through. It is more than a perspective; it is the very essence of how you operate and who you are. To shut it down, would be to shut down all parts of you, including your prosperity.

Every person, empath or not, has their own gifts. Being sensitive, psychic, or with knowingness alone does not translate to being an empath. It does not have the same challenges as an empath, i.e. like the challenge of knowing what is yours and what is not yours in emotions. Accumulating others' negative energies regularly can compromise one's health and sense of well-being. Until one learns tools to navigate energy, repeated confusion and drain can cause a person to retreat and spend excess time alone. One may try to deny who one really is, to fit in with loved ones, friends, and in the workplace (as I did several years ago), but that can make you feel out of alignment with who you really are, can stop forward progress in many areas of life, and can feel disconnected.

This book is a solid jumpstart in an empath's journey to self. As a result of being marginalized in our culture, some empaths have lost touch with what they need and want. One may become silent, existing in a bubble of sorts. This book offers tools for growth, recognizing and using your gifts, finding your voice, exploring your awakening, and experiencing the joy and wonder of being an empath.

While we all vary as empaths, many empaths experience heightened senses. You may have a pronounced sense of taste, able to distinguish ingredients in a restaurant dish where others cannot, though you're not a chef. You may hear things at a distance that others cannot hear. You may smell things like a dog can, but others cannot smell. You may see things and notice things others don't.

Seven years ago I referred to empaths as Beacons Of Light. Empaths identify with this phrase, it's caught on like wild fire, with good reason (The Awakening, Chapter 1). No matter how much you want to blend into the background and be less visible, you will still emit a bright light. It's part of who you are.

This book includes a good portion of the trainings I have offered privately for individuals and in groups. Some initial basics included in this book are: Empath Toolbox For Navigating Energy (Chapter 2). Empaths tell me this is life altering for them. Learning how your gifts may show up

(Chapter 3). Learning how to utilize your gifts can help guide you; they are part of your inner compass. It can connect you to your higher self, the part of you that knows things in advance of your conscious self, understanding more of what you need and want, solutions to problems, and inner peace. This book is an opportunity to meet yourself in perhaps new ways, getting in alignment with who you really are.

Chapter 3 explains the many reasons why self-doubt is so prominent with empaths, at no fault of their own. Confidence begins to build after chapter 3. You will learn how you can achieve a higher vibration, a high energetic frequency, whereby negative energy cannot affect you (Chapter 2).

Most empaths are old souls. Though empaths bring so much light into the world and have great compassion, as mentioned, many empaths are born into challenging circumstances (Chapter 4). This chapter is one of my favorite topics, about our soul path, soul healing and repair, life mission, life contract, life lessons, reincarnation, the Akashic Records, and manifestation.

Are you waking up to spirituality and wanting to connect with the source? Another chapter favorite, Partnering With Divinity & Your Spirit Guides (Chapter 5), offers steps you can take to make a spiritual connection with something larger than yourself, and learn about affirmations and prayers. When we do the Empath Call on this topic, it is the highest energy call of all. One person even saw a light orb in her room during the call.

Other chapters you might appreciate: Empaths & Love (Chapter 7) outlines how to bring love into your life, new ways to create and begin a sustainable love relationship, how to build on a present love relationship and long range marriage, and the magnet between empaths and narcissists, and what you can do about it. Empaths & Communication (Chapter 8), gets into such things as brain chatter, various empath communication roadblocks, with possible solutions for each. A topic that touches many is the chapter on Forgiveness (Chapter 6), why it's important for thriving and prosperity, and how to go about doing it. Then there are details on Intuition: Your Inner Compass (Chapter 9) with exercises to try. And we cannot leave out the topic of Boundaries (Chapter 10). Most empaths understandably have a challenge with, especially being that others' energies merge with ours. That chapter explains what to do with boundaries and how.

Reading the book in the order it is laid out may be helpful, as jumping to later chapters may cause you to backtrack for full comprehension. At the end of most chapters you'll find follow-up items to expand your awareness and gain forward progress on each topic, with:

- Assignments
- Affirmations
- Reference materials: books, websites, articles, videos, music

There is a new paradigm occurring that we, as empaths, are a part of. We are pioneers in the Awakening creating a new foundation for humanity, just by being born who we are!

**Chapter 1**

**THE AWAKENING**

> There is a pronounced awakening occurring since 2012. Some began their awakening earlier, some later, some to follow. An increasing number of people are seeking to access more of their mind, body, and spirit, tapping into things that native cultures, like the American Indian, and other earlier civilizations were connected with.

In the awakening you may see truth where you didn't before, all is being revealed. This can be hard to wrap one's head around. You may find yourself using more than your five senses, activated more so now than before. Synchronicities increase and may seem coincidental, but when they occur repeatedly and consistently, you will realize it is not a coincidence. You are becoming more in-sync with your own life and the world at large. Awakening may expand your sense of knowing, possibilities for connecting to a limitless source, and manifestation.

When first awakening, it can be awkward and uncomfortable, both physically and psychologically. Your body may be adapting to a higher frequency, a higher vibration, some may feel physically tired until acclimated. If overtired, I would suggest a medical exam just to rule out anything else. Some may feel the awakening as new territory, and while it can be exciting, for some it can also be scary. You may become aware of knowing things you didn't ask to know.

You may now find you want to connect to your spiritual self, not yet knowing where to begin. The more you awaken, your spirit guides that are around you at all times, may try to get your attention (see Partnering With Divinity & Your Spirit Guides, Chapter 5).

It is helpful, at the beginning of your awakening, to carve some time for yourself in sacred space, that no one can push against.

Empaths are awakening all over the world, realizing they are not crazy, but gifted, with great potential, and there are others like them. There are those that are not empaths also awakening and seeking to evolve in mind, body, and spirit. You may one day be the person others come to for help with the things that you know or you may have already begun this. People are drawn to empaths in more positive ways than 10 or 20 years ago. Every few months I hear of another famous person who comes out to express that they are an empath. We are coming together from all over the world, finding each other like never before, inspiring each other forward. It seems there are more children being born that are empaths.

**Beacons Of Light**

As an empath, you are a beacon of light in this crazy world. Do you find people stare at you and are drawn to you no matter how you try to blend in? Do people readily want to share their life story with you and unload their burdens, even strangers? Have you ever noticed when you go to an empty part of a mall, museum, or restaurant, in a short time people pile into the space you're in, it's suddenly crowded, with people wanting to sit next to you? It is the light you radiate in a dark world that others are drawn to. It is one of your gifts.

Empaths are pioneers in a new frontier. Just by being born, you are laying a foundation for a new world coming, in its early stages now. Learning about your gifts, how to use them, remembering who you truly are, is part of the empath journey.

Scientists have said our human DNA is literally an electrical transmitter-receiver. This is who we all are as humans. As empaths, this is magnified with extrasensory tuning in:

- Clairsentience: extrasensory feeling

and may include one or more of the following:

- Claircognizance: extrasensory knowing
- Clairvoyance: extrasensory seeing
- Clairaudience: extrasensory hearing

Many empaths are often not aware of their gifts and how those gifts show up. They're surprised to learn everyone does not possess the same gifts as they do, and that they vary from empath to empath. This book will help you learn more of what your empath gifts may be, how you can utilize them, how they may get you in hot water if you're not discerning, and how the experience of being an empath can feel limitless and magical at times. It's up to you where you want to take it. You've probably heard the expression: "We are spiritual beings having a human experience." Whether you believe in the spiritual or not, in God, in divinity, the source, the power of the universe, perhaps you believe there is something larger than ourselves. We have the opportunity to connect with this.

The awakening is occurring on a large scale, things are quickly changing. You are very much needed at this time.

Much of what is covered in this book will help you with steps to achieve a calm and peaceful center, with various tools.

It is my hope you will realize the greatness of who you really are and your limitless possibilities. You were not born to be a vessel for everyone else to pour themselves into. As an empath, what you bring to the planet is of great value. Once you learn more about yourself and find your voice, you may also find this time to be one of the most uplifting experiences of your life.

## Chapter 2

## Clairsentience:
## Empath Toolbox For Navigating Energy

The first and most primary thing for an empath is learning how to navigate energy, so that clairsentience is no longer a curse, but instead a door to one's possibilities.

When conducting group Empath Calls, we start each call with the below exercise. People love it and say it helps ground them, releases anxiety, clears their inner screen so to speak, and enables them to feel more refreshed to embrace the material presented. When you need to clear and ground, say at work, you can do this in just 2 minutes. If you work in a stressful environment, perhaps try it every few hours.

Grounding is important to all of us empaths, as we can feel the effects of the world, near and far. This exercise is a quick momentary grounding. I also suggest adopting a meditation practice for more extensive grounding that can often carry you more easily through the next day (detailed later in this chapter).

## Grounding Exercise:
## Breathing & Clearing Your Inner Screen

- Sitting in a chair, stretch your hands and arms up to the ceiling, like you're trying to move your shoulders up past your ears. Stretch upwards as much as you can.
- Then put your arms out in front of you, hands touching next to each other, with palms down. While remaining seated, facing-forward swing your hands

and arms as far to the right as you can, back to center, then as far to the left as you can. And relax.

- While seated pull your head down and roll it slowly to the right, back, left, and front.
- Breathing:
Did you know when you breathe into your chest, that can create anxiety all by itself?
- So now, breathe in slowly through your nose, bring the air down to your lower abdomen, stomach area.
- Let your stomach get large, and hold it as long as you can.
- Then slowly breathe out through your mouth, imagining stress and toxins leaving through your mouth.
- Repeat the breathing process 1-2 times more.

If your nose is blocked or you can't hold your breath for long, no worries. Breathe however it's comfortable for you. If you get dizzy or uncomfortable, then discontinue this Exercise and try it another time.

I suggest starting an empath journal at home, and also carrying a 3x5 inch notepad with you in transit. This way you can write down valuable things we'll cover in this book, that may come to you in fleeting moments. Writing things down will help you develop more awareness. Keeping a journal will help you chart your progress and expand your empath gifts.

It helps to connect with likeminded people wherever you may find them, such as in Facebook groups or Meetups. As mentioned, my Facebook group:

EMPATHS ON THEIR SOUL PATH

is a "closed" group where only joined members can see comments and posts in the group. Others can see only if a person joined our group. It can be very inspiring to learn you are not alone in what you experience and that others understand you. And you're certainly not crazy!

We live in a world of ever-growing static noise, world wars, plenty of bad news on TV, with fear and anxiety all around us. As an empath, you may experience 1 or all of the 4 clairs having to do with extrasensory feeling, knowing, seeing, and/or hearing. Going forward in developing your gifts and learning how to trust yourself without self-doubt, perhaps you will give yourself the gift of being a bit self-ish, in the positive, perhaps 6 months to a year of self-discovery, self-growth, self-nourishment, self-love, self-abundance, whatever it is you would like to embrace that is sacred to you. A space you create that no one else can push on. As you open to your own needs, wants, and vision, the world will literally open to you.

## Clairsentience

Clairsentience, of all the 4 clairs, is the most challenging for empaths. All people can feel other people's energy to a certain extent but are not always consciously aware of it. With empaths, we feel it in a profound and deep way in mind, body, and spirit. Absorbing other people's energies and emotions can accumulate. Learning to recognize when we are absorbing such energies, dealing with it right away in the moment, and clearing it from us daily as part of our lifestyle, can make all the difference in living a peaceful life. Once you try a few things in this chapter and see that they make your life easier, less stressful, you may feel more positive, It becomes motivating to add another thing and another. Pace yourself, there is much to learn.

7

This chapter covers a lot of information. There are some amazing tools here I pass on to you that have worked for me and a great many empaths I've trained. Different tools work for different people, so experiment to find what works best for you.

## Our Gifts

For most empaths, in the beginning of the empath journey to self, it can seem an impossible feat to distinguish one's feelings and emotions from others' feelings and emotions. In time, you can learn to separate your feelings from others, to read your feelings more clearly, understand them, embrace them, and to read others more clearly. By doing this you can more readily decide who you want to invite into your sacred space or not. This took me several years, as I had no guidance in the empath way. While, it doesn't happen all at once, those that have used the material provided in this book, have been able to release what some call the curse of being an empath (the absorbed negative energy and the accumulated absorbed emotions of others). Using the tools in this chapter, you will learn to live in your own energy, and in the next chapter can explore the wonderful gifts of being an empath.

Everyone learns at a different pace, so be patient with yourself as you grow. You will get there. Empaths are very loving people, with great compassion. Discernment is very important for us to learn.

## Empath As Rescuer

Being a beacon of light that draws others to you, one tends to take on the role of rescuer, as others frequently unburden themselves and unload their negative energy onto you, unconsciously. I've been there, done that, taken on the role of rescuer. If you are being a rescuer to people, other than a loved one who needs caretaking, people who are stuck, frustrated, unhappy, depressed, angry, in fear, and/or anxiety, and you are not trained to do so, then you may find yourself with a continued drain, absorbing continued negative energies, even at a distance. This is something empaths do a lot, rescue others, instead of rescuing themselves and growing their own lives. One can even feel other people's energy on the other side of the world.

People you've attempted to rescue, may be tapping into you and doing what I call "riding your wave." Your energy will be used up by them, because you gave it away, and left yourself behind. This is something you want to become aware of and conscious when it's happening. This is extremely common with empaths.

What many empaths don't realize is that everyone has their own soul path, their own life lessons (see Soul Path & Life Lessons, Chapter 4). Rescuing people usually doesn't work because it enables them to continue not helping their own self, and are not learning their own life lessons. If they had taken the necessary steps to seek help from trained professionals or support groups for what they needed, they would be reaching out and eventually would become empowered by their own actions.

Being a beacon of light, you will find many needy people are drawn to you, seeking that very light from you. It doesn't work like that; it's not your job. It does not belong to you and will only keep you from developing yourself as an empowered empath. As strong as the drive might be to rescue others, and difficult as it can be not to, everyone has that same challenge in life, our life lessons. We're all a work in progress. The reality is that in trying to "save" another person, it is really up to them to want to be saved and to seek help. Unless you are trained in this area, you may want to examine this type of energy drain, it's a big deal for us empaths. Perhaps you will consider some type of professional training so you can help people, have your energy remain intact, have a give and take in energetic exchange, and with that training learn how to avoid getting in the box with them. That way you would not have to lose track of yourself, or experience depletion, overwhelm, or illness. You could learn how to be disengaged with negative energy, while you help others.

You may notice that in rescuing such people, you may carry them like an emotional load on your back. Frequently, in the end, they may not appreciate it or may not benefit in a sustainable way. It's like a temporary bandage. They may want more and more, may resent you, and you may resent them. Why does this happen? Because it's not an equal energetic exchange. They are not paying for your services, there is no give and take, there is only take. Empaths often leave themselves behind in the bargain. In the follow-up section of this chapter, you'll find a post I wrote, "Hold Your Power In Energetic Exchange." This is one of our life lessons as empaths. Don't beat yourself up about it. It's a learning for all of us.

Energy, referred to in science as "frequency" or "vibration," has been validated to be part of the human experience. It can affect one's health and well-being. There are things that can feed our energy and emotions, and things that can drain us. Let's get into some of the ways we experience energy and emotional drain.

## (1) Energy & Emotional Drain – from you to you

As empaths, it can be hard to distinguish how much energy drain is due to one's own self, in thought, emotion, and how one approaches life circumstances, and how much is due to absorbing others' energies and emotions.

Building on self-growth, habits in thinking and emotions, self-talk, how one processes stress, and how one handles circumstances, all can play a part in our energy. One can learn new ways to become empowered, stronger, and raise one's energy. This is different than working on one's empath gifts. It's important to keep in mind that there can be inner challenges most people experience, unrelated to the empath focus. But for empaths, it's doubly-challenging because of the need to distinguish what is from one's own self and what is from others. In the follow-up section at the end of this chapter is an Assignment, called: Energy Check-In. It offers some clarity on where your energy drain may occur with regard to approaching life circumstances. In getting a view of your own energy drain with yourself, then when you focus on the effects of energy drain from others, it may be easier for you to understand your input to the larger picture.

Something to consider is that the stronger you become in your own self in various areas of your life, the easier and quicker it will be to identify negative energy and emotions that do not belong to you, block them, and clear outside influences that do not nurture you.

## (2)  Energy & Emotional Drain – from others to you

You're standing in a crowded subway or shopping mall. You suddenly feel pronounced emotions, perhaps: anxiety, fear, panic, tension, frustration, anger, or other emotions. You look around and notice what you feel seems to be reflected by those you see around you, whether they are people you know or strangers. You recall when you left home you were relaxed, maybe even joyful.

So what happened? Unless you're claustrophobic or agoraphobic (fear of small spaces or crowds), it's likely you've absorbed the emotions of those around you. If their energetic vibration is low or negative, like with anxiety, fear, anger, such energies can be absorbed. It can feel like your energy and air has been sucked right out of you and replaced by negative energy. Often an empath cannot distinguish how to separate what they themselves feel and what is someone else. You can absorb energies and emotions from loved ones, friends, coworkers, or strangers, even at a distance. Learning to notice what is occurring and navigating energy takes practice.

Of course, absorbing energy can be positive as well. You will learn how you can identify, clear, and block negative energy, and bring in positive energy.

If your emotion or energy suddenly changes, ask yourself – "Does this belong to me? Or does it belong to someone else?" For instance, is this my thought or emotion? Some empaths, with strong clairaudience (extrasensory hearing) may pick up and absorb others' thoughts as well, which can be complicated for you in the beginning. It does get clearer and easier as you go along. Ask yourself next, is this something helpful in my development? If it's not, write it down, and see if you can let it go. It's not your energy, not your work to do. We each have our own soul path; that's someone else's work to do, someone else's life lesson. Note it in your notepad and move on. It might take time to discern these things, maybe weeks, months. Go easy on yourself and your progress. These are life-altering processes.

## Numbing Out & Distractions

I don't have to tell you that numbing out by various means, as well as using distractions for numbing out, is very prominent in our culture. For an empath, sometimes this is the only way to stop the overwhelm, in order to function at work and in daily life. Unfortunately, it's not a remedy, it's more like a bandage that covers over and blankets who you are, including your gifts. It can block joy.

Sometimes we need to numb out and be distracted. If you need to, do it. Don't beat yourself up about this. Learning to acknowledge numbing out is enough in the beginning, while you learn more about yourself and your gifts. Validate what you feel, what you do, and learn to understand it. No one should judge you, and you should not judge yourself. Give yourself a hug and as much support as you can. And later when you're stronger, you can decide more of what you want to do. It is your life, only you can say how you will live it.

Let's touch on some ways one may use numbing out and distraction. Again, just recognizing it for now is good enough. One thing to keep in mind is that the longer you numb out and use distraction to get by, the harder it will be to come in touch with your skill set, your gifts, and to utilize them to your empowerment.

## (1) Sugar

This is one of the biggest numbing items. It offers a momentary and fake rise in energy, but drops you twice as hard and twice as low. It has detrimental side effects, like temporary depression, and can lead to diabetes. In addition, every one of us has cancer cells in our bodies, it's natural to have that. But I've read that sugar can, in some people, cause those cancer cells to grow. If up the road you choose to get off this very addictive thing, sugar, there is an old and popular book, Sugar Blues, which may help. It's listed in the follow-up items at the end of this chapter.

## (2) Alcohol

Many of us have a glass of wine or some other drink with dinner. It doesn't mean it numbs us out. For some drinking in excess may be a way to avoid feeling one's empath challenges. While it may make you feel less overwhelmed in short bite size moments, or tamper down your gifts, who you are underneath is being left behind. It can mean that your gifts, your inner compass, that might normally assist you, is being shut down. Only you can decide the degree of this and what you will do. This is all a learning, so please don't beat yourself up with this.

## (3) Recreational Drugs

Recreational drugs, been there done that, marijuana and other drugs, are similar to what I mention about excess alcohol. With excess alcohol and small amounts of recreational drugs, you may think you're shutting off absorbing negativity, but in reality it only shuts you off. What a lot of people don't realize is that it leaves you more open to absorbing negative energy. It can also open you up to negative attack and entry from negative entities. It can create extra confusion for empaths to understand what is going on. Some people use drugs to gain new insight and perspectives. New insight and perspectives can also be gained using meditation.

## (4) TV

If you watch TV a great deal on a regular basis, it can play havoc on your extrasensory tuning. Some people use it to numb out. It's very understandable in our fast-paced, stressful culture. However, numbing out with TV for many hours daily on a regular basis may also numb out your gifts. Have also heard, and don't know much about it, that it can alter one's DNA, as Wi-Fi can.

If watching TV is important to you, and you want to numb out, see if you can schedule in advance what you watch and when. I used to turn on the TV the minute I woke up and had it on when I got home from work until I went to sleep. It delivers unconscious messages, which most people don't realize. It tells everyone you need to buy something, you need to look different, you're not young enough, or old enough, or thin enough, or female enough, or male enough, you're just not good enough! TV fills people with anxiety and fear, making them feel in need and in lack, as though everyone else is doing just fine, but what's wrong with me? It's designed to do that, to keep you from your empowerment, so the corporate world has you needing and bowing down to them, instead of pursuing your own possibilities. It distracts a person in their journey to self. It can also get in the way of your progress as an empath if you fill up much of your time with TV.

## TOOLS

A lot of the tools I mention can be purchased on Amazon with good prices. Just make sure that the items have enough good reviews, and that the stones and minerals are reviewed as authentic. In this chaotic time we live in, where one paradigm of how we knew life to be is shattering, and in the background another paradigm is being created, fear and anxiety is large. As a result, 15 years ago you may have needed only one tool to clear your energy and have a peaceful unobstructed path, now I suggest using multiple tools as part of your empath lifestyle.

### (1) Raising Your Energetic Frequency

Energy is frequency, vibration. In science it's referred to as wavelengths. Light, sound, and water all travel as wavelengths, lengths of waves is how I feel it. Try picturing it like that, because that's what we send out and that's what we receive, wavelengths. Radio waves are just another form of light and wavelengths. Wavelengths are part of how you receive energy from people, including from the other side of the world. If you're a healer and you learn to tap into this energy, you can send healing to someone on the other side of the world. There's training for that by Dr. Eric Perl at The Reconnection, using healing with light, locally or afar.

In addition to receiving energy, you also resonate and send out energy. You affect your own energy level, as well as those around you. In the follow-up section at the end of this chapter is an article, "Everything In Life Is Vibration." It's not required reading. Learn one thing at a time when you're ready and test it. It's possible that many of the things in this book are new to you.

## High Energetic Resonance Tool

High energetic resonance is a tool. Learning to be in this mode of energy is like turning on a light switch, internally. Your mind, body, and spirit come alive. You can feel the energy flow through you and can't help but notice a difference. Have you ever gone to a concert that so moved you that the hair on your arms stood up. That's what high energetic resonance feels like, it's a high vibration of being. I refer to this high vibration as "goosebump territory." Throughout my day there are different things that cause me to feel this high vibration.

In addition to working on one's own inner life and approach, some things I call tools to achieve high energetic resonance, can help you hold your own energy and raise your vibration. You can learn to do this and be in this mode frequently. It not only feels amazing, but makes doing everything else that much more rewarding.

## 6 Tools For High Energetic Resonance

- Music
- Nature & Nature Sounds
- Meditation
- Love Resonance
- Partnering With Divinity & Your Spirit Guides

- Clearing your own internal path: the more you can do this, the easier it is to maintain high energetic resonance

## (1) Music

As empaths we are all about vibration, big time. To raise your energetic frequency, I suggest using music that is more ethereal, without a catchy sing-song tune. Am cautious in what I use for music as I have strong clairaudience, and am very influenced by it. If you have strong clairaudience (Chapter 3), you may repeatedly hear a catchy tune in your head for weeks. It can be like static to you gifts and can stop you from clearly picking up information you may need or want.

Everyone has different taste in music. You might like Zen music, classical, American Indian, etc. At the end of this chapter is music I use to revive after a long day's work. It clears my energy, focus, and environment, raising my frequency to high energetic resonance.

## (2) Nature & Nature Sounds

Being around nature can raise one's frequency. Placing your feet on the earth is great for grounding and centering. It can alter blood chemistry, and for some create better health readings on blood tests.

Hearing nature sounds can also raise one's energetic frequency. If you're in a location where nature is unavailable, nature sounds can be downloaded from the internet. In experiencing that "ah" moment, your mind, body, spirit relaxes, and your energetic frequency may increase.

## (3) Meditation

Meditation is one of the most important tools for an empath. It can nurture and expand progress in limitless ways. It slows one down in a positive way in a fast-paced world, relaxes, clears and releases negativity, stress, and anxiety, and accesses information using one's skill set. It can be used in partnering with divinity and spirit guides (Chapter 5).

Some of many additional benefits of meditation:

- relaxation
- centering*
- grounding**
- reduce anxiety and fear
- reduces high blood pressure
- clarity
- productivity
- health benefits
- discern what's you and what's not you
- clear unwanted energies
- cutting cords
- open the crown chakra to receive information
- tap into Akashic Records***
- build spirituality and connect with spirit
- create happiness

* Centering – calm focus physically, mentally, emotionally.
** Grounding – connects one energetically to remain present and physically connected with the earth. It reduces stress.
*** Akashic Records – book of life, of all souls, of all time (see Chapter 3).

I created a Healing Meditation process which I teach by phone and online, together with giving an Energy Reading. There are various free meditation methods to be found on the internet. For empaths, meditation is best done without music or guidance, except guidance to learn it. Otherwise the music or guidance can be a distraction to receiving information with your extrasensory skill set. Meditation can open your crown chakra, atop the head, to receive information and messages from one's higher self, divinity, and spirit guides.

Meditation has been shown to alter one's brainwaves and change brain matter in different areas of the brain that influence solution-oriented thinking, learning, memory, stress-reduction, and happiness. See article, "How The Brain Changes When You Meditate," in the follow-up section at the end of this chapter.

Adapting to a meditation practice is different for everyone, so don't get discouraged if it takes a while. For those that adapt to it immediately, it is possible they learned it in a past life. For the many empaths that experience brain chatter, at no fault of their own (due to life challenges), you may be flooded during meditating with memories, negative thoughts, or issues of the day. I call this sludge. Allow it, so you can process through and past it. When I first started, I experienced both brain chatter and sludge. It took me 3 months before I was no longer flooded with negative thoughts and memories. If you can stick with meditation, the rewards are enormous. It helps to write out the sludge and negative thoughts in your journal, to purge some of the emotional load.

Meditation can sometimes be used to figure out who you are picking up and what you yourself feel (some empaths have turned off their emotions after years of influx of others emotions). Meditation, with focused intent, can help you disconnect from and release whatever does not belong to you. In time, these things will come more naturally to you, regardless if you are in meditation or not.

I prefer meditating every night before bed. It clears accumulated energies and emotions that are not mine, any leftover negativity that didn't get cleared during the day (mine or others'), relieves anxiety and stress, and connects me to my higher self and spirit. If I miss meditating one night, the next day feels like static, it's disruptive, and does not flow as well. Some like to meditate at the start of the day to get in gear and gain clarity for a busy schedule. Find what works best for you.

## (4) Love Resonance

Love resonance is a tool that raises our vibration to high energetic frequency. What is love resonance? It is a learned thing. It is self-love, accepting who you are unconditionally, without judgment, shame, or self-blame, and then accepting others for who they are, instead of expecting others to be someone other than they are. But it doesn't mean you let everyone into your sacred circle.

When in love resonance, negativity cannot easily gain entry to affect you, but if it does it won't be there for long. See Assignments on self-love in the follow-up section of Empaths & Love (Chapter 7). That is the kind of work one does regarding inner personal challenges (it's for everyone, not just empaths).

## (5)  Partnering With Divinity & Spirit Guides

I consider this a tool for raising one's frequency, it's great for managing emotions and energy, and as an empath one can use it to up manifestation by ten-fold.  It's an important part of my daily life, for multiple reasons.  For further details, see Chapter 5.

## Stones & Minerals

Each stone and mineral has its own energy and vibration and offers different benefits.  They work with our energy in different ways.

With all my empath clients, I suggest wearing rose quartz and amethyst as soon as possible.  For me, I prefer to have my stones touch my skin as I believe that is where the most benefit is, as opposed to being encased in something like a ring.  They are crucial tools for us, for reasons noted below.

## ... 1.  Rose Quartz

Rose quartz is a pink colored crystal.  It raises your vibration from you to others, and from others to you.  It has a calming effect and creates love resonance.  It not only brings it forth in us, but brings it forth in others towards us, even strangers.  This love is a heart-opening appreciation, as opposed to a romance love.

People are usually kinder to you when you wear this stone, and you may feel kinder as well.  Strangers may be in great anger and staring at you as they approach.  As they get closer they may soften, and apologize for no apparent reason, and veer off.  This happens to me a lot.  Remember you are a beacon of light that attracts people. Everyone sees your light even if they are not consciously aware of it. So it's great that this stone can soften strangers as they approach. People will often want to give you things and be very generous with you when you're wearing rose quartz. This happens to me and clients I've referred to this stone, with similar stories of generosity shown to them, even with strangers.

## ... 2. Amethyst

This is another crucial stone for empaths. It is very important as a tool to open the crown chakra atop the head to receive information in various ways, including from spirit. It is also considered a love resonance stone. Though I've not felt it in that way, you may.

It raises one's frequency, activates spiritual awareness, and psychic intuition. I always do spiritual work wearing both rose quartz and amethyst. These two stones complement each other. Together they offer added support for a calm mode of being, relieving stress, anxiety, and sadness. I suggest wearing rose quartz and amethyst together on one wrist (beaded bracelets) or together on a chain where the stones touch your chest. I wear them all the time except in the bath. It enables me to receive more information in meditation, during sleep, and on waking.

Other benefits of amethyst are said to be protection against electromagnetic stress (cannot confirm this) and against psychic attack.

### ... 3. Hematite

This is a very powerful mineral. It looks like a metal, and comes in different colors. I used the dark gray, nearly black mineral. It absorbs negative energies so that you don't have to. The times I wore it, I immediately felt zapped, and fell asleep. I've found it works best in a carrier bag. If at work, it can be placed it in a drawer that's slightly ajar or on a desk.

### ... 4. Black Obsidian

Black obsidian also absorbs negativity, though hematite is a great deal more powerful. Unlike hematite, one will not fall asleep when wearing it, and it protects other stones you may wear.

When I lived in Manhattan and commuted during rush hour, my stone jewelry would frequently shatter onto the subway platform floor. I had absorbed negative energies of others that went into my stones. I had bracelets put together with black obsidian mixed in. They held together well and absorbed negativity from those around me.

Years later, I learned how to shield, block, and clear, so there was no build up of accumulated negativity from others. When I visit Manhattan I no longer need black obsidian and my stones stay intact, but if I lived there again, with thousands of people around me daily, I would once again wear it and also carry hematite in my handbag. There is a great deal of emotional intensity in some cities that can affect empaths. Manhattan is one of them.

## ... 5. Black Onyx

This stone balances your own negative energy, i.e. between you and you.

If you have the opportunity to go to a stone store, I highly recommend it. See what you're drawn to and what stones call to you. Try holding one stone at a time in your hand. How does it make you feel? You can then research the benefits of the stone(s) you bought. Everybody has different energy needs, and different needs at different times of one's life.

## Shielding Tools: Visualization

All the aforementioned can help block negative energies and shield you: stones, mineral, love resonance, and the various ways of raising your frequency. Then there are visualization tools to shield you.

Shielding using visualization may take practice and getting used to. It's very effective. Find a method that works best for you.

## ... 1. White Light

This shielding visualization is something I developed on my own, that works for me. I've learned several people use this same visualization. Let's say you're in the workplace or a public place, where people are spilling their negative energy and you're feeling it. First ground yourself by doing the Breathing Exercise found earlier in this chapter. Close your eyes and visualize white light all around you and breath the white light into you. Imagine the negative energy leaving through your mouth as you breathe out.  If this helps, note it in your notepad.

### ... 2.  Pink Light ~ in a Giant Lipstick Top

The next shielding visualization tool uses pink light.  I heard Doreen Virtue mention this several years ago on a radio show.  She uses it to clear negative energy.  She has an Angel Therapist show on Hay House Radio.

Picture yourself inside a giant lipstick top.  Close your eyes and picture pink light inside the top with you. Do your slow breathing, picture pink light all around you.  Now breathe in the pink light.  Imagine the negative energy leaving through your mouth as you breathe out.  If this helps, note it in your notepad.  Some of my clients prefer this visualization; I prefer the white light or steel wall.

### ... 3.  Steel Wall

More than 20 years ago, I learned this visualization from a healer.  I worked in a environment where there was a lot of negativity which interrupted my workflow.  This shielding was very helpful.  It is especially helpful if there is a particular person latching onto you psychically and energetically, with either negative or positive energy, and you want to disconnect from that attachment, to be in your energy, in your own thoughts.  As empaths, we get so used to having others' energies, thoughts, and physical senses merged with our own.  It helps for you to take time to learn how to live solely in your own energy, thoughts, and physical senses.

Say you are absorbing someone else's energy, thoughts, and sometimes physicality, though they're not in your presence, and you want to be in your own center doing what you do. They're most likely thinking of you and riding your energetic wave. Visualize a steel wall that moves around and encloses you, you hear it slam shut. Perhaps make a cluck sound with your tongue when the steel wall closes, or clap your hands together to hear and visualize the wall close. Nothing can get in. It's best not to use this all the time, as it shuts out everything else. We want to have a flow of energy and to be open to receive as well.

Years ago someone I knew was pulling on me energetically and emotionally. I did this visualization in my meditation and heard him scream in my head right as he was locked out. You may feel other people's reactions when they get locked out and should notice a difference in how you feel. After that I didn't feel his negative energy ever again.

**Clearing & Releasing Tools**

**... 1. Cord Cutting**

In my 20's I used to see auras. It is a form of seeing energy, and is one of the ways clairvoyance, extrasensory seeing, may show up in some. Years ago, I recall being with a group of friends walking on the street, of which two walked ahead of us. They were intimate love partners and I'll never forget seeing a red cord of light connecting their bodies. No matter how far one walked from the other, I could see the cord stretch as they remained attached by it. This revealed to me the validity of energy attachment.

When energy from another attaches to you, try to picture in your mind's eye that there is a cord from someone reaching and attached to you. Visualize cutting that cord. If there are multiple persons attached, I do not know if you can cut them all at once. You can try, but it may be necessary to cut the cords one at a time. Do this cord cutting with anything you feel is not nurturing and energizing you. Whatever does not make you stronger does not belong to you and you may want to consider removing it.

### ... 2. Journaling

In addition to this being a fine tool to help grasp fleeting moments of learning and messages that come to you, it can be great for releasing, and getting the sludge out.

### ... 3. Self-Talk

It helps to check-in with how your self-talk is going, as empaths often talk themselves down. Many empaths, at no fault of their own, who have felt out of place for years, may have internalized negative self-talk as a habit. You want to pay attention to this. Negative self-talk can allow others to more easily attach to your energy and to pass negative energy to you because when we have negative self-talk, it diminishes us and lowers our energetic vibration allowing for easier entry. They might feel better and you might feel drained. Becoming aware of one's self-talk creates awareness of what one needs to get clear with.

### ... 4. White Sage Smudge Sticks

American Indians have used white sage smudge sticks for clearing and releasing negative energy that may be attached to a person and to the environment. It is very effective. After smudging, you may feel more relaxed, at peace, as though a weight has been lifted off you.

How do you use smudge sticks? Some find the mini-smudge sticks and their scent more pleasing. Some prefer the larger sticks and the stronger scent. Some take the large sticks, break them up in a bowl and light it all afire. You can find white sage smudge sticks on Amazon.

I light the tip of a mini-smudge stick, hold it over a bowl so any spark will be caught, and let the smoke touch me everywhere. Then I continue through my residence smudging every nook and cranny, inside closets, and underneath the bed. Afterwards I open the windows to clear the energy out. Take a deep breath after smudging and notice how you feel. If it helps you and your environment feel stronger, note it in your journal.

For those on the go that cannot use smudge sticks, like at work or visiting a loved one in the hospital, you can use White Sage Spray. You can find it on Amazon (or may find a homemade spray in our Facebook group as one of our members is kind enough to make it for our members). You can spray it on yourself, the corners of a room or a certain area. One of my empath clients turned me onto this. She loves it and says it works well for her. A thank you to her for this great info.

### ... 5. Water

Water can be a great tool for clearing and releasing, whether it be a bath, a shower, rain, the ocean, etc.

    **i. Epsom Salt Bath.** In a warm bath you can add 1 pint of Epsom salt from the drugstore, and soak for 40 minutes. You absorb magnesium from it, which can relax your mind and body and help with sleep. It also pulls aluminum out of the body which is a toxin that accumulates from chemtrails. Aluminum can affect our gifts and our focus, as it declines the brain and memory. If you cook with aluminum pots, pans, utensils, or use aluminum foil for food storage or cooking, you might want to replace and discard them.

If you don't have a bathtub, you can use Epsom salt in the shower and scrub it into your skin. And then you can put some Epsom salt into a small plastic tub and soak your feet to absorb the magnesium. In the bath, I like to stand up and scrub it into my skin everywhere – especially the bottom of my feet, it's heavenly. Epsom salt gives you that ah release feeling. Enjoy!

**ii. Other Salt Scrubs.** There are other salt scrubs you might like and can get various types at Whole Foods in the U.S., like lavender salt, eucalyptus salt, etc. Some are invigorating, some relaxing. Both salt and water do a great job of clearing-releasing for us empaths. Enjoy!

## ... 6. Rose Water

Heritage Rose Petal Rose Water is sold on Amazon. You can spray it on yourself, near you in transit, or place in a small bowl on your work desk. It raises your frequency and absorbs negative energy. It is a great tool for empath massage therapists to use in their massage room. Edgar Cayce also recommended it for protection against negative energy.

Some say the scent is related to Mother Mary. If she is one of your guides, this may be of added value for you.

## Chapter 2: Follow-Up Items

(1)  Assignment:  Energy Check-In
(2)  My Post:  Hold Your Power In Energetic Exchange
(3)  Reference, Article:  Everything Is Vibration
(4)  Reference, Book:  Sugar Blues
(5)  Reference, Music:  re High Energetic Frequency
(6)  Reference, Website:  re Healing At A Distance
(7)  Reference, Article:  How The Brain Changes When You Meditate

## (1)  Assignment:  Energy Check-In

This Assignment gives insight into how your energy is being used up due to life circumstances, giving you your Energy Drain Average.  Up the road, you can do this Assignment again, and see if there's been improvement in lowering your drain.

Instructions:

On a scale of 1-10, how much of an energy drain are you experiencing in each of these areas, with 10 being the largest.

1.  List the # to the right of each item.
2.  Add them all up and divide by 9.
3.  Take note of what your average # is.  If it is higher than 5, it might be helpful to work on how you can lower that energy drain.
4.  When one's own energy grows stronger, two things occur.

... 1. Others' negative energies have less affect, and

... 2. You can clear and release negative energy quicker.
How much Energy Drain do you have for each item below, from 1-10, with 10 being the highest

Fill in the following:

(1) Your thoughts            _____
(2) Your emotions           _____
(3) Your state of health     _____
(4) Diet                        _____
(5) Alcohol, recreational drugs   _____
(6) Work                      _____
(7) Relationships           _____
(8) Financial Situation      _____
(9) Other Activities         _____

_____

**(2) Hold Your Power In Energetic Exchange,** Corri Milner

Empaths tend to give up their power in many ways, and weaken themselves doing this. If power is not a comfortable word for you, then use the word "empowerment." It helps to consider one's own space as sacred space, and then choose who you bring into that space.

For empaths, it becomes really important to understand boundaries, so you can better know where you begin and end, and where another person begins and ends. In this way, you can retain your sacred space, your personal essence, and your wonderful gifts in empowerment. (See Boundaries, Chapter 10.)

Something else to consider when engaging with others in any type of relationship, personal or work, is the importance of energetic exchange, to make things more equal for us. Empaths tend to take everything onto themselves including the burdens of others, as though they are responsible for other people's life challenges and how other people process their own emotions.

While we love and care for others, we don't need to take on their lives, as that is their own soul path, their life lessons. Learning their own life lessons is how each person evolves. In addition, if we do that for others, we will miss our own soul path and learning our own life lessons. Empaths tend to do this for others, while leaving themselves behind in the bargain. They often compromise evolving their own soul path in order to be with others.

Did you ever notice that when others genuinely compliment you, that you feel shy, uncomfortable, or repulsed. This is common with empaths, as one often may not know one's gifts, value, and worth. As you get to know yourself in new ways, you can take back your power, learn more of your true self, value, and worth. It's a game changer. Then you may shift to feeling the magical experience that being an empath can sometimes be, with many possibilities that await you.

Connecting with others can be done by remembering to equalize the energetic exchange -- and not have it be a one-sided thing, or caretaking (unless of course it is a loved one in need). By remembering and holding true to your sacred space and energetic exchange, you may be able to avoid feeling left out, hurt, disappointed, frustrated, and later on, resentment.

Hold your power empaths! Give your love, but don't give away your soul.

____

(3) Reference: Article:
**Everything In Life Is Vibration**, website: Altered States
http://altered-states.net/barry/newsletter463/

____

(4) Reference: Book, **Sugar Blues**, William Duffy

____

(5) Reference: Music, for high energetic frequency:
**Hildegard von bingen- O vis aeternitatis- Cantides of Ectasy sequantia- Chants de l'extase**
https://www.youtube.com/watch?v=9eFPJa95qQE

____

(6) Reference: Website: Teaches healing at a distance
**The Reconnection**, Dr. Eric Perl
http://www.thereconnection.com/eric-pearl/

____

(7) Reference: Article, Website: Mindful
**How The Brain Changes When You Meditate**, Jennifer Wolkin
**http://www.mindful.org/how-the-brain-changes-when-you-meditate/**

# Chapter 3

## THE OTHER 3 CLAIRS & 6 ADDITIONAL EMPATH GIFTS

### (extrasensory tuning continued)

- Claircognizance (extrasensory knowing)
- Clairaudience    (extrasensory hearing)
- Clairvoyance    (extrasensory seeing)

This chapter can help you discover more about your gifts. I have interacted with so many empaths that did not realize they have some or all of the clairs activated in them now, or were activated in the past, and how they can be utilized.

Most empaths, simultaneously, experience two opposite views:

(1) feel different from others and isolated, and yet
(2) mistakenly think everyone operates the same way they do.

(1) Empaths may feel they stand out no matter how they've tried to fit it, may feel treated differently, marginalized and isolated unless they have empath relatives and friends and/or have learned to navigate energy.  Some may think there is something wrong with them, or may have been told this, or were medically misdiagnosed.

(2)  In the opposite view, many empaths take for granted everyone else operates like them, not realizing they have one or more clairs activated in amazing and profound ways, that the majority of people have never experienced.  In

addition, all empaths are different in their type of gifts and intensity.

The following reflects on one's potential as an empath,

## Time Is Not Linear

Physicists say time is not linear, that it does not move in a straight line, but rather all time, past, present, and future, is altogether in one place.  That is why some people can tap into the past, present, and future to retrieve information, or in astral travel, during sleep, and in an awake state.

## Human Receptor

As mentioned earlier in this book, our DNA operates as an electrical transmitter-receiver. We are naturally built to transmit and receive information and energy.  It is who we are as human beings. With most people these electrical signals are subdued or mostly shut off. As empaths, after we learn to navigate energy and our own gifts, we can access our intuition, our inner compass, on a large scale with options for manifestation.

Our relationship with energy can be intense at times. Our internal electrical circuitry can be turned on like a light switch, may stay on, and is magnified.  Some empaths, when stressed, may affect electronics in one or more of ways:

- Computers – break down more frequently
- Cell phones – need charging in ½ the time
- Street lamps – go out when walked under them
- Light bulbs – burn out unusually fast

## Akashic Records

When our clairs are activated and put to intended use, we can gain more knowledge and inner guidance by accessing the Akashic Records.

Edgar Cayce was known as the "sleeping prophet." He would go into a trance and do readings on people's past, present, and future. From that trance, he diagnosed illnesses that doctors could not diagnose and found remedies doctors could not find. He had no medical background, yet he was correct in both diagnoses and remedies.

How did he do this? Edgar Cayce believed all information of all souls, of all time, was recorded and stored in the ether, which is referred to as the Akashic Records, also called the Book of Life. It is like a cosmic database of information on everything that's ever occurred and probable futures. See article on Akashic Records in the follow-up section at the end of this chapter.

Have you ever felt a sense of déjà vu, like you've already been somewhere or already experienced something? Have you ever had a conversation for the first time but it felt like you already had that conversation? You may have tuned into possible futures through dreams, meditation, or otherwise.

What does this mean to you? A lot. As we slow ourselves down, we begin as empaths to receive random information. This is part of our gifts. How it comes to us at the start may seem random, so pay attention if you can. You may receive information that pertains to you, to those you know, information you may need or want, or information about some place or circumstance in the world that is coming through to you. It could be knowledge about events, objects, anything.

In time, we can learn to direct our focus to receive particular information, not just randomly. For instance, we may seek to know what we need to heal in mind, body, or spirit, where to find answers to questions we may have, solutions to challenges, or knowing our next right step. These pieces of information can lead us to something further we need or want.

## Setting An Intention

Did you know that setting an intention can alter your brain and your outcomes? Dr. Joe Dispenza on a radio interview mentioned that just by contemplating: "What would it take for me to be happy?" causes your brain to grow new pathways. It sets an intention for a new outcome. He has books on how you can alter your brain and change your life.

There are no limits to where your gifts and potential may take you. You already have great gifts as an empath. What would you like to do with them?

The more we become empowered with our gifts, the more it serves us to embrace the responsibility of it, to be humble and grounded in compassion and love resonance.

Let's go through variations of how the clairs may show up. See if anything resonates with you.

## Claircognizance – Extrasensory Knowing

This is a key gift many empaths have. It is knowing something that is true, without any way of knowing it logically or with reason. This may be a large part of your intuitive mode of being.

Most people have some of this. For instance, a phone rings, you know who it is. A mother could be miles away from her child but knows when something is wrong. This would be part of the electrical transmitter-receiver mentioned that everyone has in their human DNA.

If you're an empath, this capability may be escalated. You may see someone on social media you've never seen before, but you know things about them. You just do. You might be able to write a brief profile about them from what you sense and know. This may be part of your skill set. You may think that is psychic, and yes, it is. That can be part of some empaths' makeup. Though some empaths are psychic, not all psychics are empaths. This is part of extrasensory knowing.

This knowing can be valuable to you. When you move past self-doubt and you're able to slow down the random fleeting moments of knowing, enough to grasp them and distinguish what is what, then wham! It can open doors to opportunity. It can be your inner guide to what you do or don't do, and expand on your possibilities.

## Self-Doubt

While a lot of people in our culture have self-doubt; and self-empowerment is not taught in school, I've not yet met an empath that did not have enormous self-doubt. If an empath doesn't have enormous self-doubt, then I might guess they've done inner work on their self, or grew up in a loving family that supported being an empath. Many empaths, however, are born into difficult circumstances, often traumatic, which can create self-doubt.

Self-doubt is more pronounced for empaths than most people and it can invade self-confidence. By validating and exploring why self-doubt exists to begin with, at no fault of your own, might help lessen its effects. It helps to work on removing self-blame and self-shame as soon as possible. Here's some of the reasons empaths may experience self-doubt. See what applies to you, and if you can let it go.

**Reasons For Self-Doubt**

**(1) Our Society**

In the past two decades our society on the whole has not embraced tenderness, compassion, sensitivity, and the healing arts. It mostly promotes corporations, greed, money, and fitting into a narrow mold. The concept of "don't color outside the lines" does not work for us empaths. As empaths, we live outside the lines, outside the narrow mold.
I bet you know what I'm talking about. That is where our general internal home resides, outside the lines.

With family, friends, love partners, school, religion, community, the workplace, we might be overlooked in a certain way, not fitting in with others' expectations. We may desperately try to fit in. You might pull off trying to be someone other than you are, but does it cost you more than you gain? Others' expectations in every sector of one's life,

40

i.e. expectations instead of appreciation of who you are, can create a feeling of disconnect and yes, there you go, self-doubt. It's not your fault. Recognizing this is important, so you can take the hook out of your back, it doesn't belong to you. Take your power back. You deserve to feel whatever you think, feel, and want. We're talking about validating and embracing who you are.

## (2) Too Sensitive

How many times have you heard from others: "You're too sensitive," or "you're too funny." Too funny? Okay, you've struck a chord with others that they don't know what to do with. As empaths, our river runs deep. You're not "too" anything, but rather you are a Sensitive.

This is who you were born to be. You can change the color of your hair, get plastic surgery, but nothing changes the core of who you are. It is how you operate. Let's look at it this way, it's like telling Mozart, "What do you mean you hear music in your head? Are you mad, dear man?" Now go and hear his great music and the joy that he brought to the world. Remember that the next time someone tells you you're too sensitive. If you are close to someone who tells you this, you can reply, "Yes, but you benefit from my being a Sensitive, because I understand you more than most people do." It's time to embrace and be proud of who you are.

Remember you are a beacon of light with gifts galore, you are a Sensitive. This is the very light of your being. Your gifts, together with your challenges, create your greatness.

## (3) Exposed & Castigated

This is something that trips up a lot of empaths. It certainly got me into uncomfortable situations, painful really. Most empaths go through this, and it causes them a lot of self-doubt.

You may receive information in extrasensory knowing, and are tempted to freely share it. You may have expressed to others what you knew, but it wasn't well-received. Let's go through some of the reasons you may have shared what you knew.

**1. to help** – You hoped to help someone.

**2. to be accepted and valued** – I'm not saying this is every empath. So see what applies to you. Empaths are frequently starving for acceptance. Sometimes in growing up, their families didn't understand them. This can create feeling isolated, lonely, and a strong drive to be accepted and valued by others, more so than most. As a result, you may put forth information not asked for, for this very reason, to be accepted.

**3. ego** – You may be inclined to prove to others that you have something of great value to offer. Unfortunately, this need to prove to others usually backfires, and can appear as ego. Instead of being embraced, valued, or your feeling good as a result of sharing, you might get one of these undesired reactions. See if any of these apply:

**... 1. scared of you** – Others might be scared of your abilities and try to avoid you.

... **2. see you as dishonest** – Others may think you could not possibly know what you claim to know. They may think you just happened to find out something about them from someone else or researched it. Keep in mind, they're not able to do what you do. Most people believe in what they themselves have experienced.

... **3. threatened you might know their secrets** -- When you tell others that you know things about them that they have not yet chosen to share with you, they may feel threatened by it, and wonder what else do you know about them. It can be like a spiritual intrusion. In addition, some people are not ready to deal with certain things in their own life, and may lock it up in a metaphoric internal room. Along you come revealing what they're trying to avoid in their own self; they may now feel challenged.

Empaths may find it difficult to hold back sharing knowing, and how to discern when to share. Holding back allows other people to maintain boundaries. Because empaths have experienced energies and emotions that merged with them, boundaries can be a challenge (see Chapter 10).

... **4. feel less than you** -- Others may feel not good enough in themselves, because they don't have the gift you have. They don't realize everyone has their own gifts. So for us as empaths, it's best to hold compassion. It's up to you how you want to be. For me, it took many years to realize it worked better for me and others if I held compassion and kept low-key regarding what my gifts may have revealed to me about others' personal matters. I had to work on not serving my ego or wanting to be validated and accepted in exchange for offering what I knew.

**...   5.  jealousy** –      Some people are jealous of others having something they don't have, and tend to congregate with those most like themselves.

*     *     *

To get past self-doubt, continue to explore your gifts, writing down fleeting messages of information you receive.

When you meet someone new, consider writing down everything you feel and sense about them, before you lose sight of what you knew at the start.  Do this before opening the gates and getting deeply connected in you sacred space.  Write down what you like about them, what you sense under the surface, any concerns you may have about them.  I call it a profile.

When I was younger, I wrote such things in my journal.  Because I had so much self-doubt and was starving for friends and love, even though I had a lot of friends, I would put it out of my mind, forget it, and get involved regardless.  It would come back and hit me like a boomerang, sometimes years later.  I'd go back to read what I initially wrote and sure enough, the concerns I had about a person was found in my journal, and it came to pass.  It would shatter me, taking time to heal my wounds.  If you can get clear and allow trusting what you know in the beginning, it might save you some grief.

Like most empaths, I believed in and trusted others more than I believed in and trusted myself.  Try for awhile putting yourself first until you trust yourself more and alter that pattern.  Don't leave yourself behind.

You may find that keeping up with your empath journal and reviewing it once a month, it may become your teacher. Your higher self may offer you insight in your journal writing before you are consciously aware of it. It's fascinating.

*       *       *

Let's continue further with claircognizance, as it can show up in various ways.

You're walking around in a big city, you're about to turn a corner, and you tell a friend, "Wait." You're certain you should not go on that street. In advance, you can feel dread and trepidation in your body and mind, even your breathing may be affected. That can be both claircognizance and clairsentience (knowing, feeling, and precognition). At the end of this chapter, precognition is covered in the 6 additional empath gifts.

You're driving on the highway and you suddenly have an urgent sense to change lanes, for no apparent reason. Sure enough, after you change lanes an accident occurs where you previously were, or you see an accident would have occurred had you stayed there.

I've used claircognizance to find remedies, out-of-print books, and information about a person I was involved with in an intimate relationship. I sensed someone was lying to me, and in meditation, I saw what I needed to see. That was a mix of claircognizance and clairvoyance (knowing, seeing, and precognition). It was a way of confirming what I knew. It's incredible what you can do as an empath.

If you're going to share your knowing with others, you might want to ask yourself first: "Will this be received in sacred

45

space?" If not, is this something you really want to share?

Sacred space is an honored space, that no one pushes against, so as to be spiritually open.

If you are thinking of contacting the police with something you know that you have no apparent reason to know, you might want to consider whether it will put you at risk. You could be accused of a crime.

At work you may want to help others and be included with them, by advising what you know. First, perhaps weigh if it could put you in the limelight for criticism, jealousy or fear of what you know, and put your job at risk.

**Clairaudience -- Extrasensory Hearing**

This gift shows up in many forms. You may have access to your higher self that speaks to you and may hear a voice in your head. A higher self is the part of us that knows things, often before we are consciously aware of what we know, and can lead us in higher consciousness. You may hear from your higher self, divinity, or spirit guides. It could also be from your guardian angel, someone you've known, a family member that passed on, or a spirit guide assigned to you (Chapter 4).

Do you say things to others and afterwards they respond they were just thinking that? That is clairaudience. You may be hearing other people's thoughts, whether you know them or strangers in public. Clairaudience can occur whether around people or alone. Have heard some empaths say when they are home alone, it can sound crowded.

You may receive information or messages you hear in songs. It could be messages that answer pending questions you have, or affirm something, or point you to something apropos to the moment. Right as you're thinking of someone who has passed, you may hear a song on the radio or on the internet that was their favorite, or a song you shared together.

If any of these happen frequently, you are activated in clairaudience. Everything connects us to all life and spirit. So pay attention to these things. Personally, I don't believe in coincidence.

You may hear from loved ones that have passed on. You may hear them while you're awake, when dreaming, or in meditation. Some hear their name called when they are awake and there is no one there. That is clairaudience.

You may have direct telepathic hearing with someone you know that is alive, and may communicate back and forth with each other, like a phone conversation. Later you may repeat back to each other what you heard each other say or think, and find it is accurate. Some empaths are doing this but are not consciously aware of it. Slow it down and check in with friends and loved ones so you can learn about it, and jot it down in your journal.

**Clairvoyance -- Extrasensory Seeing**

This comes in different forms as well and can be understood as "having vision." If this is one of your gifts, it is the form you want to look at, in how you personally utilize this.

## (1)  Vision – Past, Present, Future

One of the most well-known forms of clairvoyance is seeing the future.  You may see things that come true which you have no logical way to know it was coming.  That is also premonition.

Clairvoyance can include seeing in your mind, meditation, or dream something in the past, present, or future that you didn't know about, yet it is revealed to you in extrasensory seeing.

## (2)  Superimposed Vision

This is something I've experienced often, so I created a name for it: "Superimposed Vision." I see it as a gift some empaths may have.

You're in a crowd and see someone you know.  Maybe you haven't had contact with them in several years, you haven't heard from them. You take a second look and it isn't that person at all. It doesn't even look like them. It was as though the face of the person you had originally seen was superimposed onto a stranger's face.

Shortly thereafter, you learn the person you saw in superimposed vision has left you a voicemail, email, or someone you know tells you that person is trying to get in touch with you. That encompasses two combined gifts: claircognizance and clairvoyance (knowing and seeing). You had some unconscious knowing regarding this person and then you saw them in image.

## (3) Dreams

Dreams can be part of vision, whether you vision someone or something in the past, present, or future. You may see your reincarnated lives and people you have known in those lives who are part of your soul family and alive now (see Soul Path & Life Lessons, Chapter 4). In your sleep, you may even see people you will meet in the future. That is clairvoyance.

## (4) Auras, Seeing Energy

An aura is the electromagnetic field that surrounds the human body and every organism and object. Everything is alive and emits some kind of energy, including stones (and is why stones are so effective).

When you see auras, it means you have the gift of seeing energy. You may see a light emanate from other people. If you have this gift, you may want to research the colors people emanate and it's relation to health and other things. If you see auras, perhaps you could learn to give readings.

Edgar Cayce spoke of a friend of his who saw auras. This friend was waiting for a down elevator in a hotel. When the elevator door opened, he saw a group of people whose auras were blackened out, without any color to their aura. Because of this, he didn't get on the elevator. That elevator went down, smashed, and everyone on it died. He was able to see in advance, due to the auras void of color, that the life force in the body was about to die. This would be two gifts, clairvoyance (seeing and precognition).

Another form of clairvoyance is being able to see the energy that joins people together. This explains how we can do cord cutting visualizations to break that energetic   connection. There is reality to the energy fields we experience and how we experience them.

## (5)  Seeing Inside The Body

One of my previous empath clients, a licensed massage therapist, has strong clairvoyance in her own way.  I sensed she could see more than she spoke of.   Upon asking her, learned she could see inside people's bodies during massage.  But until I asked her about it, she wasn't consciously aware of it, and hadn't developed it.   This is common with empaths, being so used to their own experience, they often do not realize the gifts they possess, and may ignore them, or may experience it in fleeting moments.   Learning how your gifts show up and how to utilize them can promote your life and help others if you choose.

I gave this client exercises to further develop her gift of seeing inside people while massaging.  She began to see more.  She could tell organs that were healthy and those needing healing, by the color she saw and how things looked to her internally.  She would give special attention in massage to correspond with what she saw in each person. Regarding her repeat customers, she would often do research, providing them with helpful tips for what she sensed they needed, sometimes referring them to seek medical attention for a certain part of their body.  This was something they were previously unaware of, and after seeing their doctor, they would report back her accuracy, diagnosed with an illness in the exact area she saw a problem with, and would thank her.

The focus she gave this skill achieved results that grew her client base. She went from earning $200 a week to $200 a day in a short time, working for an employer. People quickly lined up for her services, her calendar immediately got backed up for more than a month. People were sending her cards, letters, and gifts.

It's important to know that the gifts you have as an empath is part of what the world needs. You never know where your empath gifts might take you. Every single thing we use in our skill set, whether it for deeper connection with yourself and the world at large, or in developing gifts to use in your work, you are the only one who can define what such possibilities will mean to you. It may create prosperity or may be part of your life mission. You may want to honor whatever calls to you.

## (6) Vision in Meditation

In meditation you may ask to see something and perhaps a screen comes up, it's like viewing a TV. It could be something in the past, present, or future that you see. This is clairvoyance.

One's gifts can change. When in my 20's, I had a teacher who saw a TV screen in her meditation, and though I meditated then, I didn't see it. It was twenty years later that I did. You just never know how your skill set will change.

## (7) Visual Symbols & Messages

Some people see symbols or messages at appropriate times that point them in the right direction, to something they need or want. It may come to you in articles you see at just the moment you need it. It may come to you in symbols you see of things that are personally close to your heart or in number sequences that have messages attached to them (for number sequences, see Chapter 5). Seeing things at just the right time you need and want it, is a clue that you are in alignment with yourself, in-sync with your soul path and being on track. It is also referred to as synchronicity, something revealed to you right as you seek it. That seeing is clairvoyance.

In the awakening, synchronicities happen more frequently, and is part of manifestation. People call it coincidence until they see it happen repeatedly as part of their lifestyle. That's when they realize something has altered in their life. They have awakened.

*   *   *

If you do out of body travel (also called astral travel), you may see and hear things while visiting others' homes in astral travel, that can be validated by others that you've traveled to. Of course, I believe in caution with out of body travel not to impose on anyone by viewing someone's private life, unless they invite you to. In my heart and mind, that is a psychic invasion and against spiritual principles. This astral travel with seeing and hearing is a combination of clairvoyance and clairaudience (seeing and hearing), and extrasensory travel.

## 6 Additional Empath Gifts

### (1) Animal Empath

All empaths can feel animals, after all we are clairsentient and feel every being deeply. However, an animal empath has a telepathic connection with them, and may communicate with animals and them with you. You may hear what they are thinking, needing, wanting, can understand them, and they understand you. As an animal empath you may find animals in people's homes that avoid everyone else (sometimes even the humans they live with), but will seek you out, maybe even come lay on you, and may share information with you psychically about their history. The animals can feel-hear you as you can them. You can interpret for them.

### (2) Flora Empath

A flora empath has great connection with plants and flowers. There can be 2-way communication between a flora empath with plants and flowers. It is more than a green thumb. You will find that not only do you know what all plants and flowers are needing to thrive, but may be able to help them prosper to grow faster and larger. They respond to you, they feel-hear you as you feel-hear them. A flora empath can provide plants and flowers with a sense of well-being.

### (3) Geomantic Empath

A geomantic empath has the gift of reading energy from the earth. You may read what the earth is telling you in the moment, or may read what is coming. One might predict earth disasters and even know of earthquakes at a distance.

## (4) Medium Empath

A medium empath has the gift and deep connection of feeling, seeing, and/or hearing those that have passed on, with loved ones or strangers. That is the traditional definition of a medium empath. My thought is that this may also extend to feeling, seeing, and/or hearing spirit guides, and not just ghosts.

Have you seen the TV show Medium. The main character in the show, Allison DuBois, is a real person that the show is written about. Ghosts have provided her information which she was able to relay in order to solve murders and such. She has several books.

## (5) Psychometric Empath

A psychometric empath has the gift of feeling energy from objects and sometimes reading objects, objects that have been used before by other individuals, like clothes, and photographs. Some photographs can be read by empaths that have strong clairvoyance. Some empaths that have brought objects home that belonged to others may find they are overwhelmed with sudden emotion or negativity. A psychometric empath can pick up and absorb the residual energies that were left behind by the past owner(s) on the object. It might even affect the health of a psychometric empath. In such a situation after discarding such objects, it is best to do a white sage smudging of you and your environment to clear energy (see Chapter 2). For such empaths, after discarding the object and then clearing you and the environment using smudging, negative emotions and body symptoms are resolved.

I think this may be why some empaths need to clear their stones before using them, as they can feel the previous energy attached to the stones of others that have handled them. In 25 years of using many types of stones for various benefits, I have never cleared my stones and had no issues. It may be because I am not a Geomantic Empath, though sometimes I can read photographs. In my instance, that would be clairvoyance.

## (6) Precognitive Empath

A precognitive empath may know things before they happen. It may come to them in meditation, a dream, sensing something, or in knowingness. This is part of what is mentioned earlier in this chapter regarding sensing danger before walking on a street or changing driving lanes to avoid an accident.

Precognition can also involve positive things, like knowing something great is coming your way and about to happen and it does, knowing you are soon to meet the love of your life and you do. This precognitive experience could be a combination of any or all of the 4 clairs: clairsentience, claircognizance, clairaudience, and clairvoyance.

## Chapter 3: Follow-Up Items

(1) Assignment:  What is Your Primary Clair?
(2) Reference, Article:  Akashic Records: The Book of Life
(3) Reference, Movie:  Evolve Your Brain
(4) Reference, Article:  Auras & Auric Fields

(1) **Assignment:  What Is Your Primary Clair?**

Doreen Virtue says we all have one primary clair and the other clairs supplement that one clair.  In my humble opinion, I believe this may vary per person, and that some may have a mix of their clairs equally strong and activated.  See what is primary for you and what clairs are presently activated in you.

This Assignment is found online and is also in Doreen Virtue's book below.  The book is a great read and helpful to all empaths and lightworkers working in the service of others.

http://www.healyourlife.com/the-four-clairs
**The Angel Therapy Handbook**, Doreen Virtue

(2)  Reference: Article, website: Edgar Cayce's A.R.E.
**Akashic Records – The Book of Life**
http://www.edgarcayce.org/the-readings/akashic-records

(3)  Reference: Movie: Dr. Joe Dispenza
**Evolve Your Brain: The Science Of Changing Your Mind**

(4)  Reference: Article, website: Be Your Inner Light
**Auras & The Auric Field: 7 Auric Bodies**
http://beyourinnerlight.com/auricfield.html

# Chapter 4

## SOUL PATH & LIFE LESSONS

This chapter explores concepts that may be new to you. They are part of my belief system. I cannot prove most of what I mention, nor can I prove the existence of God or my spiritual faith. These are personal things we each adopt into our belief systems. See if anything resonates with you.

Physicists of our time question whether form creates spirit or spirit creates form? I don't have all the answers but I do have questions.

### Soul Path

Are you living on your Soul Path?
What is the definition of Soul? In part, the dictionary reads:

> "The spiritual or immaterial part of a human
> being or animal regarded as immortal."

Also:

> "The principle of life, feeling, thought, or action in
> humans regarded as a distinct entity, separate
> from the body."

I believe before we are born, we take part in creating a life contract regarding what our life mission here will be, and our soul purpose. I.e., why we're here and what we're meant to do. When we get here, most of us forget and may spend a good part of our lives trying to figure that out.

As empaths, we're usually old souls, and are such as children. I believe we have one soul that goes from life to life in reincarnation, with that soul being reborn into a new body. In each life we learn new things, develop ourselves in our gifts, experience challenges, and attempt to master life lessons. It is a way of evolving from life to life until we grow to higher resonance vibration , unconditional love, in understanding our self and others, enabling us to manifest quicker in each lifetime.

We are born as empaths with extrasensory tuning, bringing so much light into the world, and possessing abundant compassion for others. I believe this is who we are due to having evolved in many lifetimes. Why are empaths born with extrasensory tuning, able to tap into energy and emotions of others? How did this happen? I believe that as one's soul evolves in soul continuance from life to life, one's gifts grow, learned skills and knowledge are accumulated and carried over into the next life. We bring all that we have learned to the world now. It involves unveiling and remembering who we truly are.

Each of our soul paths is different than anyone else's. While one may have commonalities, share a home, love, family, with others, your soul path has to do with your own evolution, and what you've learned or didn't learn in reincarnation. One will keep returning to learn the same lesson(s) until it is understood, then will move on to the next thing in one's evolution.

For many years, I lived with a man who would ask me these questions:

    (1) What is your life purpose?
    (2) What are you doing with your life?
    (3) What is important to you?

My answers were, "Huh?" I didn't have a clue to any of those answers. I was like a leaf in the wind. Where the wind blew, I went.

I was disconnected from myself, from others, from my life journey, and from my soul path. I didn't know what I wanted. I was in therapy for years and yet I had no answers about my life. I got lazy and disengaged with life in general. I lived vicariously through others. There was not much meaning there for me. Several years have passed since then; seems like a lifetime ago. The answers to those questions above are vivid in me now and they ring a bell in my very soul.

This is what a soul path is about, i.e. your soul journey. The journey takes place on the inside and reflects what you do on the outside. Your journey may differ from others in your life, even your love partner, and it usually does, because your soul path may be different.

What would it mean to you if you could see your challenges and struggles as life lessons, and that those life lessons could have an advantage to your life? If you could view your challenges as tools to learn about yourself and the world, and have them be stepping stones in your evolution to empowerment and greatness, what might that feel like?

We evolve to what we are ready for. The question is:

How do we find balance, wholeness, and allow the very essence of who we are, to open doors to our possibilities?

Okay, that's a 4-part stacked question! Really, how do we find balance in a world that is so out of balance, so fragmented, and distracting us from those possibilities?

Here's the thing: If we **allow** our life circumstances to be our tools and our teachers, and if we **choose** to look at our circumstances in that way, as tools and teachers, it changes the dynamics. Our challenges can sometimes be viewed as our greatest gifts, when we realize where they take us in our journey. Did you know that some talented healers discovered they had healer capabilities only after a severe trauma? Would you say the trauma was a gift? Maybe....

Granted, we cannot have control over everything in our lives, and there may be things we don't understand. But what we do have control over is how we choose to unveil our life. If we open ourselves up to new perspectives, and allow ourselves to let go of assumptions that don't really apply, it can offer us new insight. If we spend our time wisely, more wisely than we spend money, honor who we are, nurture ourselves, and love ourselves, this help us to open and perhaps get a glimpse of who we are on our soul path.

## Life Lessons

What if you could look at your challenges as purposeful, even as gifts? I'm repeating this on purpose. Let's say life lessons could be evolutionary tools in learning. One may not see challenges as gifts in growth until later on when the results of where those challenges took you become obvious. If that challenge didn't occur in the way that it did, the road you traveled might have led you elsewhere.

What if everything happens for a reason? Why does there have to be a reason, you may ask? I thought of that too. This perspective changed in me several years ago when I experienced a trauma. I found myself saying to friends quite unexpectedly, "This is happening for a reason, it's purposeful, as awful as it is now, it will be a benefit. I just don't know what the benefit is yet. And I have faith that in time I'll learn what that benefit is." It was a pretty severe trauma and I had challenges that continued because of it. And my gosh, yes, I did learn what the benefit was. Over and over I would later discover the purpose of each challenge and it's benefit. Each mountain I had to climb internally and externally brought me somewhere of value.

I'll share some of my story here in the hope you might be able to explore your own story. During an oral cosmetic surgery, I was required to take a medication in order to proceed. Though I was in good health prior, the medication caused internal bleeding in my gut that I could not control on my own, though I tried for a long time. It created a serious illness that brought me close to death. After being in bed for several months, with no improvement from day to day, I felt I had to decide whether I wanted to live or die. It turned out to be one of my life lessons.

Through that illness and the physical and emotional pain of it, I found my soul, which I had lost touch with, due to childhood trauma. I found my inner wisdom, which I didn't know I had, through internal digging into my core self at that time. What else did I have to do lying in bed for several months? This inner wisdom is something each person has. Even if you are unaware of it at the moment, it resides within you.

So there I was at a crossroads of life and death, I knew it. I decided consciously, yes, I would live. This choice I made, and this is a choice each of us has to make in our life at some time or other, sometimes multiple times. No one else can decide for you what choice you will make; it's part of one's life contract, one's soul journey.

After choosing life, I told five medical specialists that I would overcome the illness and then get off the cancerous pharmaceutical, a medication that had me walking into walls. I chose to follow my inner voice, not the medical specialists who spoke of doom and gloom and more medication I said no to. Though all five doctors told me I had to stay on the medication for life, I knew otherwise, my inner wisdom told me. I told all of them, "You just watch me, I'm going to overcome this, and I'm going to overcome it my way." They were all stunned when I recovered, healed, got off the pharmaceutical, and X-rays then showed no sign of my ever having an illness. I recovered from an illness they told me I could never recover from. The specialists said they never saw that happen before. I did it through mind, body, and spirit. I needed to heal in all 3 areas, and I did. It was hard work, but I did it to get my life back.

Sometimes we come to a place such as this in our life because our mind, body, and spirit is not "with" us, so to speak, but rather disconnected, fragmented, and in need of healing. And so, things happen in our life, like with health, that reflect a broken link, a disconnect on the inside.

Here is the surprise. When I built my life back, I wound up building oh so much more than was in my life before. I had opened a floodgate of understanding, connectivity to myself and spirit, and to the very life source, to whatever you refer to that as. I had never felt so connected to life as then and since. What I had learned was a feeling of self-acceptance, unconditional love, and joy.

So where did all this come from, this connectedness, joy, and unconditional love? It came from my life lesson, which turned out to be forgiveness (see Chapter 6). My life lesson was in forgiving multiple people, from my childhood to the present, as well as forgiving myself. It allowed me to open doors and to feel consistent joy and unconditional love for the first time in my life.

After forgiving others, my healing began and continued rapidly after that. It wasn't magic. When you're in bed so long you have time, but then again this can be done with focus, even if you have a busy life. In growing up, I had moments of joy but not every day, it was few and far between, less than it should have been, though I had a very active life and many friends. My life before my illness was as though a blanket had been overlaid onto it, a blanket that darkened my vision, which I could hardly see out of, and that disconnected me from the world. It was like the world was gray, metaphorically. And in this life lesson, at the crossroads of life and death, I brought my life from a dark place to one of light, which focused on revealing, learning, expanding, self-acceptance, unconditional love, and feeling joy. And that's why I became a life coach to help others do the same in their life. This is a learning process for each of us.

During that time when I was recovering, I considered something I never thought of before. I heard it from others, and it immediately rang true for me in my very soul. It may be hogwash to some or it may call to you. As the expression goes: one man's ceiling, is another man's floor.

**Life Mission, Life Contract, Life Purpose**

Here is the concept. As mentioned previously in this chapter, before we are born we have a choice to choose our life mission. It's also called life contract or life purpose. We sign up for this. It's part of our soul continuance on our soul journey from life to life. It is believed that the soul travels in reincarnation from life to life, with a similar purpose. And that it continues until completion of that soul.

When we're born, we usually forget our contract and life purpose, until we slow down and listen to our inner knowing. It took me to get very ill and face death before I slowed down and began to listen. Some of you may get there sooner, and blessings if you do, either way.

In my learning forgiveness, then learning unconditional love which followed, I was able to experience my own soul repair; the soul repair that caused me to reconnect to my life and to all life. It was in that soul repair that I realized my life purpose. My life contract is to serve others, to help others from their darkness to their light, to find their joy, passion, inner peace, and motivation, all in a troubled world.

Part of my life contract also involved being born to parents that were cruel and abusive, physically and emotionally, it was very hard. Many empaths are born into difficult circumstances, perhaps traumatic. I knew the darkness, but I learned to bring it to the light. In learning this, it became my life mission to help others do the same. Had I been born in different circumstances, I might not have the skill set I have now or the understanding of how to process it. I might not have understood people and been able to help them evolve in their lives in the way that I do now. My process directly reflects my journey. It's different than other life coaches in what they do. So that's my life contract. I let go of self-judgment and my life truly launched.

## Reincarnation

Some people think that you cannot remember reincarnation. Some children remember, until they're socialized and taught otherwise, and then they forget.

Reincarnation can be rediscovered. It takes paying attention, slowing down to hear, think, feel, and see the signals, and connect the dots. I've been slightly odd in that department, as I've remembered past lives since I was 4 or younger. It was frightening because I would go out to play and be snapped out of being in the present to a past life, and didn't understand what was happening. I would go to some other landscape and see it out of my eyes instead of where I physically stood, and there was some other person there with me. It was as though seeing this other place overlaid onto the environment, simultaneously. Vivid memories. It was like living in 2 worlds, at least. I never discussed it growing up, didn't know what it was, and learned about reincarnation only after starting college, stumbling upon books in the school library that I wasn't looking for.

How do you remember a past life? Well, you start with things that are familiar to you for no apparent reason, that you haven't learned of by reading or seeing it somewhere, you just know of it. Because some empaths tend to know things they have no rational way of knowing, with regards to what you sense it could be one of your past lives. It is helpful to find three connections you may have to affirm each particular reincarnation.

Regarding past lives, it's helpful to research certain things you hear or see that may be familiar for no apparent reason and they call to you. The clue is if it feels familiar, like "going home." There are certain countries, cultures, foods, music, literature, art, books, etc. related to certain lifetimes that you feel familiar with, drawn to, and might not have been introduced to, or hardly at all. Usually there are repeated instances that speak to you, giving clues that this may be a past life. You may know of cooking recipes you've never learned or seen, yet you know how to make exotic dishes with all of the ingredients. That has happened to me. That's usually a sign of reincarnation. Again, it's best to find three ways to connect with each reincarnation.

There are many other signs you can look for. Try going to a museum with exhibits of ancient civilizations, like The Metropolitan Museum of Art in New York City. When walking through any of the ancient cultures housed in the large rooms there, see if you get any sensation. You might even hear music that no one else hears because it's coming from inside you in remembering, or you might remember something else. You might see tools or clothes or jewelry that looks familiar to you from an ancient time. Again, it's like going home. Whatever you see and you connect to, do research, pursue it. There are no coincidences in what resonates with you. It's part of your soul journey.

You can use meditation, with the intention that a past life be revealed to you. Once you are used to doing meditation regularly and it feels more natural to you, you can ask divinity and your spirit guides (see Chapter 5) to show you your past lives. It can occur in that meditation space I refer to as "the zone," a state of being where one's brainwaves alter, and you are neither awake or asleep. Then pay attention in the following days, weeks, months, for information that may come to you and call to you. Be patient, it may take time and a number of tries to access information if you're not used to it.

You can also try freeform writing. For this, the conscious mind can trip you up with self-doubt. So I suggest bypassing the conscious mind by writing as fiction, and allowing anything that comes into your writing randomly, to emerge onto the page without censorship, judgment, or editing. You can also ask for help with your freeform writing, if you are partnering with divinity and your spirit guides. They may download information to you in writing, in dreams, or in meditation. In the beginning, you may feel like you're making things up, and that's okay. It may very well be related to reincarnation and is why it is occupying your mind in the first place.

## Soul & Reincarnation

Frequently, there is a recurring theme in the soul that continues. As we learn and clear our life lessons, there is another item to consider here. As mentioned in Chapter 3, physicists say that time is not linear, but rather is all in one place, i.e. past, present, and future are all linked together. Otherwise, how could one remember a past life? How is it some children can give exact details, names, addresses, and everything about a past life and it can be found out to be exactly true? How is it some people can see the future?

How many people sensed the 9/11 tragedy before it occurred or dreamt about it?

How is all of this possible If we consider past, present, and future to be joined together, it makes sense. So if we consider the physics of time being all in one place and relate it to one's soul, does it make sense that what one experienced in a previous life and in this life, goes on after this life in soul continuance?

**Soul Path & Life Lessons**

If you're having a challenge in your life right now, ask yourself: What can I learn from it? How can it benefit me, though I might not see it right now?"

Here's a story of a woman I coached and a life lesson that redirected her to her soul path. She worked in the corporate world and earned a high salary. She traveled frequently and spent money like water without thinking about it. She saw herself as "entitled."

She told me there was a man on the bus who would try to sit next to her, to speak with her. One day he asked her out and she blew him off in a condescending way. She told me, "How could he have the nerve to ask me out? Can't he see I'm well-dressed? He's wearing poor workman boots and they're all worn out. How dare he ask me out." Are you cringing right now? Who knows the courage it took that man to ask her out. Her reaction was as though entitled.

Life lesson? We're going there. She lost her high paying job, a job that had her wrapped up in illusion. Entitlement is an illusion, it is an attitude of disconnect from self and from the life source. Behind entitlement is pretense, usually emotional pain, discord, and lack of joy. Though she tried for a long time to get a new job in her industry, she found nothing, and went through her pension. She lived high on the hog, thinking she was entitled, until she ran out of money. She couldn't pay her credit cards, and couldn't borrow any more money from the bank or from friends.

She filed for bankruptcy and had to start anew, moving from where she lived her whole life. Entitled? Not really. Her life lesson? Compassion for self; compassion for others. When stripped of money and a middle class lifestyle, in her alone, quiet moments away from distraction, she connected to herself, her inner wisdom, and spirituality, for the first time. She got in touch with her emotions, did affirmations, and learned meditation. She learned that the challenges she had faced, the losses, the bankruptcy, was a life lesson. She discovered she had healer capabilities she never knew of before. She began a new career and created a new lifestyle. A career that rewarded her with solace and joy.

When asked, if given the opportunity would she return to her entitled life, she answered no. While she learned to respect money and the mobility it afforded, she said she would not go back to that lifestyle of entitlement. She viewed it as barren instead of the lush new existence she created. She connected to her life contract, her life mission. Could things happen for a reason, even if there are harsh losses? Had this challenge in her life not occurred, she might not have gone in the direction she did, i.e. to be a healer.

Where there are challenges in one's body or brain that cannot be changed, that is different than a life lesson. In such an instance, one can find the greatness of who they are and the abilities they have brought into this life, which may be a part of their life contract. Such a person may be an inspiration to other people, may offer something others get to experience, need, or want, or offers others a purpose. Find that special something you have, it's there. Everyone has value.

Why do some people come into our lives for a long time and some for a short time? When people leave our life, move away, change, or pass on, we tend to blame ourselves. What did I do wrong, one may ask? We may see death or a person's departure from our life as dark. It does require grieving; we all experience that. There are some losses that cannot be replaced.

When there is a departure, a loss of a person in one's life, what if it could be viewed as part of that person's soul journey on their soul path? We each have a soul path. What if before they were born they had a life contract, and their mission here was one of short duration on the planet? What if they returned to their celestial home to where their soul rested, to their continuance of their soul work and learning. Is that our fault? Is that something we can blame ourselves for? What if their soul was here for a certain length of time, and they were done with what they came here to do? How can we honor their soul path, without torturing ourselves?

The gift of knowing someone here in this life can end when that person either completes their desired mission in this life or they veer off in life on their soul path that no longer merges with ours. It can be at no fault of our own. Blaming ourselves or demanding something else of others only creates suffering.

Here's an example of a woman I coached. She was frustrated in most areas of her life, her vision of her life was vivid but unfulfilled. Anxiety and roadblocks in various things were affecting her. One of the roadblocks was her love relationship with a man she lived with for several years. She blamed him for things; he blamed her for things. The relationship lacked understanding, hearing, acceptance, and negotiation. She learned that their life paths were so very different. Sometimes this can be worked through, but in her instance she came to the realization that she could not fulfill her own soul path while in that relationship. Staying with him required giving up her own soul path, her life contract, her mission.

When she came to this realization, she blamed herself for being in such a position. But blame doesn't work, it's a judging of one's self. Eventually she saw the gift of what she had acquired in that relationship, as there is something to be gained in everything. She gained a new understanding of herself and others. And in that particular relationship she understood they were simply on different life paths, which conflicted. She came to understand this life lesson for her was: not to blame and judge herself, not to blame and judge others, and to trade it in for understanding. That was her life lesson. She removed fear that was involved, her motivation catapulted. She then embraced her soul path totally with no blame, in compassion, and moved on.

And so some life connections last a long time, some a short time, but they all have value, and something we can learn from each connection. All have something to do with each person's soul path on their soul journey, and one's life lessons. Until we learn a particular life lesson, sometimes we have repeated, unwanted experiences.

## Soul Continuance & Soul Groups

I recall something that occurred when I was a teenager which remained vivid in my memory. While meditating back then I had an out of body experience and found myself out in space. It is there I saw teardrop shapes of light. These teardrop shapes were on their side, traveling together in groups, a bunch of them. I instantly thought of them as spirit in light form, soul groups traveling between lives. Why did I think that? I don't know, I'd never heard of such a thing; hadn't heard or read about souls or spirits, yet the memory of it stayed with me.

Did you ever meet someone for the first time and both instantly felt you already knew each other. I believe we travel from life to life in reincarnation in soul groups, and meet again in other lives. You will most likely meet again with people from past lives in this life, and/or in the next life. It can be someone you were married to in a past life that you meet again now, and could be different sexes in this life. Or a parent could die and be reborn a child, with their previous child now being their parent. This is what I refer to as soul continuance on our soul path (soul path consisting of one being that is reborn into different bodies, different circumstances), and in one's continued soul group. In this soul continuance, we meet people again in different lives, different roles, different relationships. The more you meditate on these things, they more they unfold. It's part of our learning, resolving something from a past life that didn't go well, completing, wanting to revisit someone or something from a past life, could be part of our life lessons, or all of the aforementioned. There could be many variations in our soul continuance.

A soulmate can be a love interest or a soul connection to a friend, animal, or family member. A soulmate helps us to evolve in some major way and touches us deeply, and vice versa.

## Soul Murder, Soul Retrieval & Soul Repair

There are some things in life that can cause damage. I've heard it referred to as "soul murder."

When a child is beaten down physically or emotionally they can become fragmented, perhaps broken. They may be told or made to feel they are worthless, dumb, or less than. That is soul murder.

In Nazi war camps, prisoners were known to grow attached to their destroyers and would volunteer to help the Nazis torture and kill other prisoners. The tortured and killed prisoners experienced soul murder, as did the helper prisoners experience a death of their own soul, as they moved into soul murder of others.

On a lighter note, but still damaging, when one places others in a position of being worth more than one's self or matters more than one does, when what others think and feel is more important than what one's self thinks and feels, this is a type of soul murder of one's self. This soul murder of one's self mimics how one was treated and learned to be. Anything we learn can be unlearned, and done otherwise if we choose. We are all a work in progress.

Can one heal from this? I believe, yes. I know a person who experienced soul murder, did heal from it, and is living now in wholeness. There are some souls that have been damaged in a past life, which may be brought over and affect one in this life. There are people that work with this. It's called Soul Retrieval and Soul Repair.

On a slightly different note regarding Soul Continuance from a past life, I coached a woman on this, though it's not something I learned in coaching school. From the start of our coaching relationship, I noticed her coughing for no apparent reason. She had no cold or illness and didn't know why she was coughing. Her medical exams revealed nothing wrong. I kept hearing in my head "reincarnation." She came to me for business coaching to start a new business. The business she was starting was as a medium. Every time she'd think, speak, or engage with anyone about this new business, she would coughing intensely and start to choke.

The book "Many Lives, Many Masters" by Brian Weiss. M.D, is fascinating. The author is a therapist who unexpectedly found a number of his clients had past lives bleeding into their present life, affecting them in the now. This occurred so much, that eventually his practice was filled solely with this type of therapy.

So here I was coaching a client and sensing she needed to revisit a past life that was getting in her way in this life. She was unaware of what was happening to her and had no control over the coughing and choking. Having heard an interview with Dr. Weiss and how he conducted his sessions (I'm not trained in this), we tried an experiment together in reincarnation regression.

In that reincarnation regression here is what she recalled for the first time. She had a past life during the time of the Knights of Templar, closely tied to the Crusades and forced religion. She was a medium in that time, that's what she did for a living. The church members saw her profession as violating the church. They brought her onto a large ship, put a rope around her neck, and threw her over the side, dangling her from the rope. That's how she died. After this was revealed to her, her coughing and' choking mostly resolved. She would thereafter only cough when she felt threatened by someone or something (even if it was an assumed threat and of no consequence). Soon she was quickly able to identify what was going on when the cough would occur, and it would immediately resolve. She had remembered what she needed to about that past life and her part in it, and how it entered into this life in soul continuance.

So how do you recreate your life when you feel you need soul healing? There are different ways to go about this. I reference below some practitioners who help people in the area of soul repair, as well as some reading material on the soul. If you or someone you know have experienced soul loss, there are those that can help with soul retrieval and soul repair.

## (1)  Hank Wesselman, Ph.D. & Jill Kuykendall

This married couple are shamans that have done workshops on soul loss and soul retrieval. Hank Wesselman, Ph.D., is an anthropologist, with fascinating books. Jill Kuykendall is a registered physical therapist and transpersonal medical practitioner. To find a description of the symptoms of soul loss on their website, **www.sharedwisdom.com**, go to the top right tab and select - Shaman Healing - Soul Loss. One of their quotes:

"People can lose parts of their soul due to traumas such as abuse or the loss of a loved one. Or when a child is born into this world and the first thing they perceive is that they are not wanted or that everyone was expecting a boy and they came in as a girl. This can create a form of Soul Loss that can affect a person throughout their life."

Jill Kuykendall enters into the spiritual realm. There she conducts soul retrieval and soul repair for those who sense they were damaged or missing part of themselves.

## (2) Dr. Bruce Goldberg

Dr. Bruce Goldberg is a dentist and hypnotherapist. Have heard several fascinating interviews of him on radio. He's highly spiritually developed and works on soul healing and energy healing with individuals, using hypnosis and altered states of consciousness. He trains people by introducing the unconscious mind to the higher self, what he refers to as the Superconscious Mind. One of his quotes:

"When we love ourselves enough, negative energy patterns will dissipate and the body will eventually heal itself."

## (3) Ian Lawton

Ian Lawton has a book on the soul. One of his quotes:

"Everybody has a soul that preexists their existing life and almost all of us have previous lives before this."

He recounts that children have memories of past lives, the details of which have been proved true. He writes that humans are here to experience and grow over many lifetimes.

## (4) Deepak Chopra

He writes:

> "As a human soul, you can play infinity of roles and the physical being is like the printout of the soul."

He also writes:

> "By getting in touch with the hidden dimension of our existence we can reach greater contentment in our lives."

___

## Chapter 4 : Follow-Up Items

(1) Assignment:  Soul Questions
(2) Reference, Book:  Many Lives, Many Masters
(3) Reference, Website:  Shared Wisdom
(4) Reference, Book & Website:  Soul Healing
(5) Reference, Book:  The Big Book of The Soul
(6) Reference, Book:  The Book of Secrets

___

## (1) Assignment:  Soul Questions

See what comes to you.  Took me several years to figure out the answers to these questions, so go easy on yourself.
Just planting a seed is enough for now.

... 1. What is your life purpose?
... 2. What are you doing with your life?
... 3. What is important to you?

___

(2)  Reference, Book:
**Many Lives, Many Masters**, Brian Weiss, M.D.

___

(3)  Reference, Website:
Hank Wesselman, Ph.D. & Jill Kuykendall,
**www.sharedwisdom.com**  Click the top right tab on site,
select: Shaman Healing - Soul Loss.

___

(4)  Reference, Book & Website:
**Soul Healing**, Dr. Bruce Goldberg,
http://drbrucegoldberg.com

___

(5)  Reference, Book:  **The Big Book of The Soul**, Ian
Lawton

___

(6)  Reference, Book:  **The Book of Secrets**, Deepak
Chopra

# Chapter 5

## PARTNERING WITH DIVINITY & YOUR SPIRIT GUIDES

Some of us may want to connect to something larger than ourselves. We may refer to this as: God, Goddess, Divinity, Ascended Masters, the Source, the Universe. Many find this type of connection expands who one is, offers more meaning, peace, emotional and physical healing, manifesting what one needs and wants, and a deeper level of connection with people, spirit, and all things.

Because there are so many ascended masters one can choose to connect with, for simplicity sake I refer to divinity. It's best if what you connect with calls to you or sparks you. Only you can say what feels right for you.

### Manifestation

"Manifestation" has become a popular word. While there may be varied views of it, I refer to it this way:

> **"What you go towards, comes towards you."**

It may sound simplistic, but there are inner and outer steps that go with manifesting. The above concept works; I see people manifest what they want all the time. It is my belief that in each life we get better at manifesting, a result of accumulated learning in our soul continuance.

As one develops their empath gifts (Chapter 3), manifestation may occur ten-fold when utilizing those gifts on a regular basis. As you learn to embrace more of who you are, move past personal impeding challenges, and get unstuck, you may manifest more quickly. When you start to see things appear before you that you were thinking of or seeking, at first you may think it's a coincidence. It's synchronicity that occurs more frequently after awakening. It's part of manifesting what you need and want. When using one's empath gifts, you may receive messages from your higher self and spirit guides, both of which can help point you to your next right step. Manifesting also requires working on one's personal life, internally and externally. It's a mix of these.

Have you seen the movie "The Secret"? After seeing that, you would think you simply make a wish and it happens. It takes more of us than that. The movie can help you think about what you want, set an intention, and create a vision. Then with inner work, one can move through and past obstacles, negative self-talk, and take action steps.

A lot of people don't think about this self-talk, i.e. the voice in one's head that gets a person stuck or talks them down. In coaching, we call it a gremlin, it's a block. And there are other internal blocks we have like: assumptions, limited beliefs, and misinterpretations. And then there may be blocks in how one relates to money, fear of failure, or even fear of success. These are other topics entirely different from our empath topics, but important to consider when speaking of manifestation. While some of one's gifts may appear magical at times, what one focuses on, one's thoughts, one's inner gremlin that talks a person down, and the actions one takes or doesn't take, are all part of the picture. None of these can be left out if one intends to manifest.

Manifestation is a part of my connection with divinity and spirit guides. I like to connect with spirit daily, whether I'm in need or not; it has become my spiritual family, part of my lifestyle.

## Why Connect To Divinity?

What is your connection or relationship with divinity, if any?

Most people are taught by religion to view divinity as a parental figure and they are "the child of God." This creates a dichotomy of the almighty God that is out of reach and us small, diminished humans. While "almighty" seems fit when describing divinity, as it is all-life encompassing, so much larger than ourselves, I prefer "partnering with divinity." In partnering, you have some say in what you want and how you want it. Many religious people don't consider or allow themselves that say. You will often hear things like, "it's in God's hands," or "only God can determine how this will turn out." And while I do believe that to some extent, when you embrace what you want and how you want it, you have a better opportunity of achieving it. Your will, your wants, your voice is of great relevance and importance. A lot of people don't consider this. You can design your life and step into the life you've designed. I see people do it all the time.

Many religions tout their God as a God of fear. You've heard this, right? It's perhaps easier for religious institutions to control the masses through fear. But what if you viewed God as a "loving God"? Well, for one, you'd probably be thrown out of the church and told not to come back. I know people who were told that in different churches, different denominations.

Partnering with divinity may seem like a radical idea, but It's a way to become stronger in making decisions, taking action, and directing your life in partnership with a force much larger than yourself. It creates more responsibility for the steps taken in your life, rather than blindly handing it over or melting into the background like wallpaper. This is where we get to step up and step out to join divinity in partnership.

Several years ago I decided I wanted to serve divinity and prayed saying aloud: "Please allow me to serve you and to hear you." This was my daily prayer for 7 years, until I heard back a voice in my head that wasn't my own. The voice I heard said, "You can serve me starting right now by being kind to strangers." I've been hearing divinity ever since. It was divinity that prompted me to start the Empath Group Program, my Facebook empath group, Empath Calls, and this book.

You may have a different mission in this life than I, but regardless of what it is, it is important. You too can partner with divinity and your spirit guides, ask for what you want, how you want it, and pay attention as it unfolds.

When I first asked for a sign to know that I was heard by divinity, I was not a spiritual person. I had no idea how to pray or to connect with spirit or to receive messages or signs. I was just beginning my spiritual quest. You may very well be further along than I was. For me, it was worth the wait to have that connection. Some empaths I've coached have made a connection very quickly in hearing and even seeing divinity. It blows my mind. You may be more advanced than me in this, time and practice will let you know. You may choose to connect with a divine source that is not referred to as God and you may have a name in mind for that source. Whether you choose God or another source, whatever you choose is the way for you.

Meditation can open your crown chakra to be more receptive to messages from divinity, received however your empath gifts come to you (this varies). The crown chakra is our center for trust, devotion, inspiration, happiness, and positivity. It's also the center for deeper connection with ourselves and a life force greater than ourselves.

Connecting and partnering with divinity can raise your frequency, your vibration, and can help heal one's pain in mind, body, and spirit. We all experience pain at some point in our life, but suffering is optional. (Suffering from physical pain all the time is a different matter entirely.) If you seek help with something that pains you, it might be useful to offer that up to divinity, release, and let it go. Write it out, say it aloud, ask for help, let your burdens get lighter until you are relieved of the weight. If you cannot do it on your own, it's healthy to reach out for support, in addition to divinity. There is no shame in this, and is why chief executive officers and coaches go to coaches and counselors. When one releases their pain, spontaneous joy may be experienced. For some, the entry to joy and freedom is through divinity.

I light candles every day, one for divinity, and one for the archangel that works with me. I thank divinity for being with me when I light that candle. Then I thank the archangel for being with me when I light that candle. An usual thing happens with these candles. The light of the candle reacts to what I ask, having nothing to do with air or wind. For instance, I may ask divinity a certain question, and the candle flame will nod forward, that's a yes, or sideways, that's a no. There have been rare occasions where the candlelight moved about in extreme and frantic motion. That's usually to do with something harsh occurring.

## Who Is Your Divinity?

If you're not sure who your divinity is, you might start with research on the internet. This has proved fruitful for a number of people I've coached. Here are some key search words you can use: God, Goddess, Divinity, Ascending Master. You can type your search for any of these and then on the search line, you can add a plus sign and type the name of a country your divinity may be found in. An Afro-American man I coached did a search for "divinity + Africa." He found the name of a certain Goddess in Africa that immediately resonated with him, her name felt familiar for no apparent reason. When you connect with divinity, it may feel like going home. Say the name aloud. Does it resonate with you? If no, move on to the next search.

## Meditation & Divinity

In meditation, you can ask who your divinity is. One empath client did this and heard a name in her head, a name she'd never heard before. Upon searching the name on the internet, she learned it was a foreign and ancient God's name. Different empaths may receive information in different ways. You may hear it in your head in meditation, in a dream, or in your waking state. You may see something on the internet or in a book and it resonates with you. Or someone may mention it to you out of the blue at just the time you are seeking this information.

Meditation is a great way to connect with divinity. At the start of each meditation, you can ask divinity to join and protect you. I used to have unwanted out of body experiences repeatedly, which scared me and caused me to stop meditating for many years. Then I started to call on divinity. Now I feel protected and rarely have out of body experiences.

In meditation, you can call on divinity with: "tell me what I need to know," or "show me what I need to see." In time, you may learn what divinity or your spirit guides, including angels, are telling you. You may get visions of the future. You can ask divinity questions about things that matter to you. You can ask about a certain person. Of course, I'm not talking about psychic invasion of others. Years ago I was involved in a love relationship with a man that I sensed was seeing someone else. He said no he wasn't. I had a feeling otherwise. So in meditation I asked divinity to show me what I needed to know about that. With my eyes closed, a screen appeared as though I was watching TV. I saw him with an Asian woman, looking at her, his face intimating more than a friend. Sure enough two weeks later he broke up our relationship to begin one with the woman I saw in meditation. How information comes to you will depend on the following:

## (1) Practice

The more you meditate, the easier it can be to open up and partner with divinity and spirit guides. As mentioned in an earlier chapter, I suggest meditating without guidance or music once you've learned how, as it can get in the way of realizing your gifts and receiving information. You want to allow connecting to spirit without distraction.

For those empaths new to meditation, some experience what I call "sludge" in the beginning. Some empaths have brain chatter, under it is sludge. Brain chatter is common with empaths, a consequence of challenging circumstances from early on in their lives, and it comes into one's daily process of thinking and feeling. It surfaces regarding memories that are not yet resolved or healed, or leftover issues from the day. As a result, some empaths may be delayed in achieving what is in this chapter until the sludge is allowed to come up and out in your meditation. Perhaps start writing all the sludge stuff in your journal book to give you insight as to what's going on and what might be getting in your way. In time, you will be able to get into the zone where you can receive information in meditation. We can also receive information on waking and in days and weeks that follow.

Though when younger I experienced brain chatter and sludge, especially during meditation, the 3 months it took me to get in the zone was well worth it. Most people I've taught healing meditation to by phone, get in the zone in days or weeks (much quicker than I did).

Meditation can reveal new things to you but can also reduce stress and anxiety. Try to keep doing meditation regardless, as it's a great discipline that can help ground you, and can lead you to achieve things beyond imagination.

## (2) Open To Receive Information

Receiving information can also depend on how open you are. Self-doubt can get in the way of focusing, or receiving information in fleeting moments. When self-doubt lessens, when one feels an element of self-protection, and is living in their own energy instead of being bombarded by others' energies and negativity, it becomes easier to receive and grasp information. I do protection and clearing which helps me open to receive, mostly by wearing gemstones and meditating daily. Sometimes I add pray and affirmations. Find what works for you.

Go easy on yourself. We are used to quick fixes in our culture. This is not a quick fix, but a tool you can learn and use for a lifetime.

## (3) Your Skill Set

Your particular empath skill set will determine how you receive information. As you use your gifts more and grow spiritually, you may develop new skills. You never know what skills are going to develop.
Here are some examples of questions I've asked divinity and received answers. Practice trying your own questions and see how that goes.

... 1. I was living in Manhattan's upper eastside and wanted to move to a nearby different building. I found an apartment and building I liked but because I used to spend money frivolously, I didn't have the 3 months rent deposit. It was a higher rent than I was used to, so I asked divinity in my meditation where could I get that money. I woke up the next morning hearing an immediate answer in my head: "Call the management agent. Tell him you know he wants this apartment, he should make you an offer, and you might move."

When I called the management agent, without missing a beat he asked how much I wanted. He immediately faxed me a contract to sign, and said he didn't want me to change my mind. That week he hand delivered a check with the set amount, and I moved to the apartment I previously saw and liked.

... 2.  Another example: I wanted a specific out-of-print book, before I ever used the internet.  I asked in meditation where I could find it.  On waking, I heard in my head to go to a bookstore on a specific corner downtown.  Sure enough there was a used bookstore at that location that I didn't know of. The person at the counter said they didn't have the book.  I went right to the shelf, retrieved and bought it.

There can be magical moments in being an empath when partnering with divinity.  You can use this for whatever it is you're seeking, large or small.

**Spirit Guides**

In the follow-up section at the end of this chapter are two links, articles on spirit guides by James Van Praagh. I highly recommend his events.  I attended one, with an audience of 1,000 people, he guided us in a visualization, picturing our self going up in an elevator to meet our spirit guides.  I met mine. In my mind's eye I saw my spirit guide, heard his name, saw him working in a glorious garden.  He spoke in French, which I don't, but communicated telepathically.  As this exercise was so many years ago, I cannot recall the details of how James Van Praagh conducted the exercise, but it was very effective. My spirit guide was a go-to spirit for me for years. You may want to check out James Van Praagh's books.

Some spirit guides may have been with you on your soul path from previous lives.  You can ask your spirit guides in meditation what you want help with, what you want to know.

Pay attention to what you hear and see in meditation, on waking, and in the days, weeks, and months that follow.

Sometimes during meditation, with my eyes closed, I see images that move very quickly and can't always decipher them. It can depend on the length of time I spend in meditation as to whether I can get clarity on what I'm seeing, allowing time for it to emerge. Sometimes they look tribal or like symbolic pieces of art.

If you have something important you're working on in meditation, perhaps you will do meditation additionally at a time when you're not tired. That way you can stay with it long enough to gather more information. Sometimes information may come to you when you are coming out of the meditation. See if you can jot down information that starts flowing to you, no matter how odd or irrational it may seem. Perhaps keep a journal or a tape recorder nearby, to note what comes in fleeting moments. Up the road it might make sense. On waking in the morning, try to loll in bed for 10 minutes, do some slow, deep breathing, and gather what comes to you. It could be information about people in your life, information about you, your work, things in the world, past lives, your present, your future, your next right step, anything. Then pay attention thereafter.

Guardian angels may be near, looking after you. Some say they are loved ones that have passed on. A guardian angel in the bible is defined as a heavenly spirit assigned by God to watch over us throughout our lives. I don't know which it is or if there are both. I know someone who believes her father became her guardian angel when he passed on. In most of her family photos, an orb of light is present, which she believes is her father. A lot of people say these orbs of light are spirit. It could be guardian angels; it could also be other spirits, including other-worldly spirits. If you see orbs of light, pay attention to what you see and feel. Does it feel like good energy, or not? What messages are you getting, if any?

If you want to communicate with a guardian angel that is around you, a loved one that passed on, you can write a letter to this person and leave it out where you felt their energy most in your home. You can ask them to come into your dreams and meditation to communicate with you.

It is said angels are always around us and that we receive messages from them all day. We might not notice they're communicating with us because it may be in unexpected ways. Depending on which of the four clairs are activated and your skill set, the angels may communicate through these related skills.

Doreen Virtue is an Angel Therapist with an Angel Therapy show on Hay House Radio. She hears from angels all the time and says we each have at least two spirit guides with us. She refers to them as angels or archangels. The leader of archangels is Michael, the healer of archangels is Raphael, and there are others. You may see statues of them in Roman Catholic churches, as well as visual cards and pendants.

I'm not sure that hearing from spirit is always from angels, and believe messages can come from a variety of sources. When any spirit is trying to communicate with me, I am only open to it if it feels healthy, good and coming from love, and I call on divinity to be with me for protection.

Something to keep in mind, that because we have free will, it has been said divinity and spirit guides cannot assist us, unless we ask for their help.

Here are some ways you might receive messages from divinity, your spirit guides (including angels), dependent on how your empath gifts come to you. Below are categories of how I experience these things in detail. See what resonates with you as you start to learn of your spirit guides. I highly suggest reading Doreen Virtue's books. Her Angel Therapy Handbook is an amazing guidebook for empaths and light workers who work in service of others.

## (1) Divinity, Spirit Guides & Clairsentience – In Feeling

You may be busy going about your day and your emotions suddenly shift to feeling a high vibration of energy, love, compassion, and joy, for no apparent reason, and you didn't feel that before. For me, it feels like a cool healing light, a circuitry of energy that runs through me, energy that feels different than my own. It gives me goosebumps, feels very good. I sense this is divinity or spirit, as it happens so suddenly, and appears to come from outside of me. Sometimes I will have this occur when I'm focusing on something and wondering if something is true and then will be flooded with this cool healing energy, which feels to be an affirmation from divinity that yes it is true.

When one partners with divinity on a regular basis, you may be filled with wonderful, sudden energy that energizes, heals, and has a loving vibration. When we are in tune with ourselves, we get to know what is our energy and what is coming from elsewhere. It feels very supportive when we receive such energy from divinity or spirit.

Sometimes spirit communication can be from a ghost, whether you knew them or not. Once when visiting a woman in Manhattan, I suddenly smelled a very strong scent of violets which wasn't there when I arrived. She hadn't put on any perfume. I asked if she knew anyone that died, affiliated with the scent of violets. Yes, her mother had worn violet perfume every day when she was alive. And then I heard a message to relay.

You can distinguish when a ghost is nearby. The air around you will suddenly turn colder, and a presence can be felt. However, when I felt divinity or a spirit guide around me, the air did not feel colder, and felt suddenly that light and energy was filling me up. A ghost's energy can be felt outside you. Divinity or a spirit's energy can be felt inside you.

You can also be visited by a living person. I felt the spirit presence of someone enter my apartment and due to smelling by a particular scent, knew who it was. The next day I asked him if he did out of body travel and did he visit me, he said yes. I do not recommend ever doing this without permission. It is a spiritual violation.

Spirit is a powerful thing. It can be of divinity, those who have passed on, spirit guides, elements that have never been human, like angels, spirit of those presently alive, or spirit of otherworldly beings.

## (2) Divinity, Spirit Guides & Claircognizance – In Knowing

Many empaths receive information in knowingness. You may suddenly know how to fix something electronic though you're not electronically inclined. That might be assistance given from archangel Michael, who is skilled in that way. You can ask him to help with your computer.

You may get a great idea for a new invention, service, or product that did not evolve from anything you were thinking of, but just appeared out of nowhere as though downloaded to you. Where are these messages coming from? Perhaps some brilliant inventions came from divinity or spirits of those that passed on. Sometimes these things come from outside one's self, but sometimes they come from you, your higher self, your empath gifts tapping into knowing, and the Akashic Records (see Chapter 3).

In addition, when you start to open up you might access things from reincarnation. I've done this with recipes I just happened to know without having any way to know them, before I had the internet. One day I went to a small Chinese grocery store in the back roads of Chinatown, in Manhattan. I brought various ingredients to checkout counter. The Chinese cashier looked at me perplexed and asked why I was buying such things. I said, "Why of course to make Lotus Root Soup and Winter Melon Soup. These are the correct ingredients, I'm not leaving anything out, am I?" "Yes," she said, "they are correct. How did you know?" "Reincarnation," I answered.

### (3) Divinity, Spirit Guides & Clairvoyance – In Vision

You may have vision and see things in your mind's eye in your head, in dreams, with your physical eyes in signs or symbols that appear before you, flashing or sparkling lights. You may see orbs of light, moving objects, repeated number sequences, or articles on the internet that call to you and answer the questions you're thinking at that moment, on topic.

Years ago I lived in an apartment with long windows covered by long white sheer curtains.  A woman visited me and the curtains suddenly began to move in a fashion I'd never seen, rapidly as though blown by an air conditioner or fan, but there was neither and the window was closed.  In addition, a flood of blue light ran through the curtains as they moved.  I asked my visitor if she saw these things, "Oh yes," she said, "that's Archangel Michael, that's what he does.  He goes where I go."

## (4)  Divinity, Spirit Guides & Clairaudience – In Hearing

Another way messages can come to you is through sound. Have you ever heard your name called while awake, with no one around? Ever hear spiritual sounding music out of nowhere?  Or a warning from a disembodied voice?  Think about it.

You may receive wise words that come to you in writing and speech, that sound foreign to your thoughts, as if it came from elsewhere, and is downloaded to you.

You may hear a high-pitched sound or ringing which may be spirit trying to get your attention. (One should see a doctor to rule out any medical issues.)  I used to hear the sound of a toy telephone ringing; no one was around me had such an item. I knew that spirit was a certain person's father that passed on.  He used to visit and communicated each time in that specific way.

You may hear a conversation in your head, yet there are no people around you. It could be divinity or spirit. It could also be clairaudience of psychically hearing people you know, wherever they may be. Some empaths have experienced this, called friends, and learned what they heard in their head was true, it was said aloud by someone that wasn't present, but was heard nonetheless ninety miles away or on the other side of the world. Practice, in time, will enable you to better decipher what you are receiving.

In terms of spiritual connection, how we receive information and communicate has to do with our level of frequency (vibration), i.e. in what we're capable of receiving. As the frequency of divinity is usually too high for most people to perceive, angels can communicate on behalf of divinity with us. Angels have a frequency lower than divinity, higher than humans, but they can lower it still to meet our energetic resonance and communicate with us. Their doing this allows us to feel them and to receive their messages.

You may have heard the word "ascension." It has different meanings. For some, the term ascension might simply mean higher consciousness in spiritual awareness. For others, it could mean you reach the place of meeting all ascended masters (i.e. all divinity) in meditation. This is a very high consciousness. When you have reached that, usually you have a capacity to see the future, and may meditate and achieve what is called a "light body" in your meditation. Those that have achieved light body in meditation have sometimes astral travelled to what is called the Celestial Sphere or another realm, The City of Lights. I have not done this, but have known of those who have.

## Prayers & Affirmations

Prayers and affirmations set an intention. The difference is that a prayer is between you and something outside of you, something larger than you, i.e. divinity, the source, the universe. Whereas an affirmation is between you and you. It is a reprogramming of self.

Asking for what you want may be new to you and may take getting used to. Many of us have lived mostly like a leaf in the wind, with whatever came to us. You may think one can only experience a life or character traits you were born to. The reality is that at any given moment you can decide this is not how your story will end, and take steps to create the life you want. It begins with a thought, then a vision, and action steps, while removing inner and outer obstacles. It's a strategy that works.

## Prayer

A prayer is your inner voice asking for assistance in what you need and want, taking action in partnering with something larger than yourself, i.e. divinity, spirit, the source, or the universe.

In the beginning of my awakening, I wanted to pray but didn't know how. So I worked with a book of pre-set affirmations, "The Prospering Power of Love," by Catherine Ponder. The author calls them affirmations, but they're more like prayers because they ask for something external, something outside of one's self. Many swear this book has helped them in achieving things. By focusing and repeating the affirmations in the book, it is like willing it to happen. You can also try calling on divinity to assist for added possibilities. This book helped me to figure out how to pray and to create customized affirmations. It's a good start.

You can create your own prayer with divinity in partnering together. It takes practice and getting used to. There is no right or wrong way. Write to divinity whatever it is you want. See if you can give it detailed focus, be specific.

A coaching client was used to praying to God most of her life in whatever prayers the church taught, but she had never personalized it for herself. A recent circumstance had caused her to revisit grief in the loss of a loved one who died years ago. It triggered heightened sadness and pain, so heavy-weighted, it was tiring her out, and making her feel badly. Understandably, grief is something we all go through, loved ones cannot be replaced. We focused on her partnering with God, and for the first time she created a new prayer. She asked that God help carry the pain and heaviness and lift the emotional burden from her. In just days she felt quite different. Alongside grieving and sadness was a predominant feeling of peace and joy. The emotional weight was not so heavy. She attributed her sudden new feelings as direct input from God in partnering together.

## Affirmations

An affirmation is between you and you. It sets an intention that when repeated often enough is absorbed, reprograms your brain, and becomes part of your very psyche. Sometimes one has an overlay of what one should be, think, and do, which can unconsciously drive one's metaphoric car to its outcomes. I call this a template. I.e. we're not driving our metaphoric car, the template is. It can create outcomes we don't consciously want, repeatedly. Affirmations can help to alter that template for a re-set more aligned with who one is and what one wants.

For example, say you felt you don't have love in your life, and your inner gremlin voice, as we call it in coaching, says you're not loveable.  An affirmation might be:

> I am loveable.
> I resonate love.
> I attract love to me.
> I am as I should be.

In doing an affirmation, it should be customized and personalized.  In creating it, one needs to take into account what you are trying to overcome in what happened to you which created the present gremlin voice that gets you stuck or talks you down, and to replace that voice.  It should be aligned with who you really are or want to be now, and the outcome you want to achieve.

An affirmation may sound trivial, but they work deeply and profoundly regarding one's inner self in one's psyche.  Then that inner self connects to outer outcomes. It effects manifestation.

The best way to do an affirmation is to start with doing only one. There are two ways of absorbing it:

(1) writing it, or
(2) saying it aloud.

You can do either, or both.  Writing it 15 times a day can be lengthy but productive.  Typing it doesn't work; people don't absorb it that way.  When saying an affirmation aloud I prefer to do it right before sleep, as that is when I feel vulnerable and most apt to absorb it.

My clients say they have best results saying the affirmation aloud because it involves emotions, which one can feel resolving during the process. If writing it is too tedious, you can print and tape it to the back of your cell phone or some place you will see it throughout the day. When you are done with an affirmation, i.e. it is now part of you, you should see a difference in your outcomes.

Have done affirmations for several years. It helped me in many ways, and caused me to reinvent myself. It changed my life in ways I wanted it to: in the way I thought, felt, and behaved. If you're not familiar with prayer, affirmations can more easily lead you to prayer, and to your prayer with divinity. It's a helpful practice. There are several affirmation books on Amazon to choose from.

## Symbols & Messages Received

Our angels that work with us try to get our attention. A common way that they communicate is through symbols or number sequences. It could be with symbols that mean something specific to you, so pay attention to that.

Angels may use number sequences to connect with you. You will see people on Facebook frequently speaking about numbers like: 11:11, 333, 444, 222, and other number combinations. In the follow-up section at the end of this chapter is a link to Doreen Virtue's Angel Number Sequences. If you don't see the number combination there, you can do a Google search for the number combination "+ angel message" for different interpretations found. You may see repeated number sequences on the internet, your clock, addresses in your travels, license plates, store receipts, time when emails are received or sent, etc. In seeing these numbers, take note if the same number combinations happen repeatedly in the same day or on a regular basis. There may be a message for you to pay attention to.

Your angels may also show you symbols in a dream. You may see symbols on the internet or wherever you go, you may repeatedly see a symbol or name. One empath client was searching for her spirit guide. In her meditation she heard the name Gabriel, the name of an archangel she had never heard of. She asked Gabriel for a sign to affirm that she was one of her spirit guides. She then dreamt about a harp. The harp had no place in her life up until that moment. She later learned that the harp was a symbol for Gabriel. It was a confirmation for her.

Some people see feathers or coins. When this happens on a repeated and regular basis, and sometimes in the most unlikely places, it's a sign that one's angels are around them. You may find feathers wherever you go, in your home, and where there may be no birds. One woman bought a wooden bed frame. Days later she found an angel carved into the side of it, where none existed on delivery. She also found feathers in her Manhattan apartment on a regular basis. When young, I found feathers wherever I went, including indoors. Now I find coins.

## Asking Your Angel For Help

There comes a time in everyone's life that one might feel between a rock and a hard place, needing outside help. In addition to turning to divinity in your time of need, you can also turn to your angels. I've done this only two times in my life, and each time I had results.

Perhaps you've tried to resolve something to no avail. You might be in grave need. You can ask your angel to speak with the angel of a certain person. I learned this from "The Prospering Power Of Love" book. You write a letter to your angel and ask your angel to speak with the angel of a certain person. In your letter, explain the situation in detail, be specific about what you need help with. And see what happens.

After I wrote the letter, I folded it inward, placed it under a tall candle in glass and let the candle burn (of course only when awake and at home). You can have the candle burn every day until it is completed. And see what happens.

I'll give you two examples of how this worked for me, several years ago.

(1) I had a life and death illness, was on sick leave from work three months, when my doctor suddenly declined approving further disability benefits, unless I paid an extra $1,000. Having already paid him several thousand dollars, I was unable to pay the additional sum. I was forced to return to work while still frail.

On returning to work I was met by new management, who immediately removed me from my 14 year position and the senior team I loved working with. Instead, I was immediately placed at a different desk to work for twenty demanding newbies right out of college, all competing to prove themselves in the corporate world. A demanding bunch. There were many different computer programs for their department that I was not trained on, and was unable to keep up. My new supervisor was angry and said if I was too sick to keep up and do everything required, I should just go home and stay there. That would mean no disability benefit, no unemployment benefit, nor the health insurance I desperately needed at that time.

That night I wrote a letter to my angel to speak with the supervisor's angel. The next morning at work the supervisor came over smiling at me, acting pleasant. She reached deep into the inner pocket of the desk I was moved to the day before, which was not yet cleaned out. She pulled out a ceramic angel, stood it on my desk, and said, "I love angels." Then she said, "Don't worry, I'll get someone to train you on all the new programs, you'll get the hang of it, and if you need extra help, I'll get some of the girls to help with your work," and she walked away. This was a direct result of asking my angel for help, as I don't believe in coincidence.

An hour later, a young executive was standing at a printer near me, asking me to fix a printer jam. The printer was gray colored inside and outside. When I opened the printer to fix the jam, inside the printer sat a small orange monarch butterfly. It jumped onto the top of my hand, sat there for 3 minutes, while the executive and I looked at each other speechless, and then flew around the bend. Get this: I worked on the 50th floor of a building in a concrete city, Manhattan, a building where the windows did not open. I worked at that building and other buildings like it for 20 years, and never heard of a butterfly in such a building.

I went to lunch that day with an office colleague. I didn't tell her about the letter to my angels or the office happenings, but did tell her about the butterfly that came out of the printer and sat on my hand. She said, "You know what that was, don't you? That was an angel," she said.

I trained on the programs and continued to work there until I was much stronger, no longer worried, thanks to my angels!

(2) I had just moved to another apartment in Manhattan (a different apartment than previously mentioned in this chapter). I paid a broker fee of several thousand dollars, plus 3 month's rent, plus 3 movers. Right after I moved, I was laid off from my job, the job mentioned above. The broker had lied when he said the club below my apartment was a quiet club and closed every night at midnight.

It was so loud the floor moved. The gun headphones did not shield the blasting music, which sounded as loud as a stadium every night 10pm to 4am. The broker would not return my fee, the landlord would not return the 3 months' rent, and Manhattan's Department of Housing investigators were backed up at least 6 months. After two weeks the sound took a toll on my body. My back went out for the first time in my life, and I walked hunched over like a cripple. I feared another month of such noise could cause me serious damage.

I called someone I knew to ask for a loan to move, he said absolutely not. I knew him a long time, he was someone who never changed his mind. That night I wrote a letter to my angel to speak with this man's angel. The next morning I awoke to find an email from him that asked for my check routing number. He wired me thousands of dollars in 30 minutes and said I didn't need to pay him back, so I could move. I moved that week.

These angel experiences were precious to me beyond words.

_____

**Chapter 5 : Follow-Up Items**

(1)  Reference, Article: 4 Ways Your Spirit Guides Are Trying To Connect With You
(2)  Reference, Article:  A Guide To Your Spirit Guides
(3)  Assignment #1:     Look For Your Divinity
(4)  Assignment #2:     Look For Your Spirit Guides
(5)  Reference, Book:    Angel Therapy Handbook
(6)  Reference, Book:    Ascended Masters
(7)  Reference, Article:  Angel Number Sequences
(8)  Reference, Book:   The Prospering Power of Love
(9)  Reference, Video:  Edgar Cayce:  Fairies, Angels & Unseen Forces

_____

(1)  Reference,  Article:  **4 Ways Your Spirit Guides Are Trying To Connect With You,** James Van Praagh
http://www.healyourlife.com/4-ways-your-spirit-guides-are-trying-to-connect-with-you

_____

(2)  Reference,  Article:
**A Guide To Your Spirit Guides**, James Van Praagh
http://www.vanpraagh.com/a-guide-to-your-spirit-guides/

_____

(3)  **Assignment #1:  Look For Your Divinity**

... 1. Via Meditation.  In meditation, can ask for your divinity to show you who they are, tell you their name, or point you in the right direction.  Pay attention to what you hear and see in the days, weeks, and months that follow. Did you come up with anything?

... 2. Via Internet.  Can search on the internet for - Divinity – Gods - Goddesses - Ascended Masters.  Can be a divinity from now or from ancient times, in any country.

Can also do a search with one of the above words "+ [insert country]" for divinity in that country.  Did you come up with anything?

When you find the name of a divinity, try saying it aloud. Does it resonate with you?   Does saying it feel good to you? Is it familiar or is it like going home?  If not, move on, and try seeking another.

## (4) Assignment #2:  Look For Your Spirit Guides

...  1. First read, "A Guide To Spirit Guides," noted in (2) above.

...  2. Via Meditation.  In meditation, can ask your spirit guides to show you who they are, tell you their names, or point you in the right direction.  Pay attention to what you hear and see in the days, weeks, and months that follow. Did you come up with anything?

...  3. Via Internet.   Can search on the internet for spirit guides (archangels and others) in any culture, country, or time in history.  See what resonates with you.  Did you come up with anything?

When you find a name of a spirit guide, try saying it aloud. Does it resonate with you and feel good to you?  If not, move on and try seeking another.

(5) Reference, Book: **Angel Therapy Handbook**, Doreen Virtue

(6) Reference, Book: **Ascended Masters**, Doreen Virtue

(7) Reference, Article:
**Angel Number Sequences**, Doreen Virtue
http://spiritlibrary.com/doreen-virtue/number-sequences-from-the-angels

(8) Reference, Book:
**The Prospering Power of Love**, Catherine Ponder

(9) Reference, Video: **Edgar Cayce: Fairies, Angels & Unseen Forces**
https://www.youtube.com/watch?v=tIQvEjnAbfc

# Chapter 6

## FORGIVENESS

(1)  What can you gain by forgiving?
(2)  What does unforgiveness cost you?
(3)  How can you tell if you need to forgive?
(4)  What steps can you take to forgive?
(5)  How do you know when you've completed forgiving?


Out of more than 1,500 Facebook posts I've done, it was my post on forgiveness that drew the most attention by far. Many people have a need for forgiveness, but it is something rarely explored.  Where are you with forgiveness?

### Forgiveness vs. Unforgiveness

Should you forgive or not?  Some think forgiveness is about changing other people's behavior or receiving apologies.  It is more about you than about others.  It is about taking back the wheel of your metaphoric car and driving it, rather than it driving you.

Unforgiveness can sometimes be a strong motivator in "fighting the good fight."  You've heard that expression, haven't you?  Fighting the good fight can perhaps pump you up, but at what cost?  What if holding onto unforgiveness costs you peace of mind and being diminished in love, health, or abundance?  What would be the gain of unforgiveness then?

One may think they are projecting unforgiveness outward, perhaps hitting back so to speak, but you may instead be at the effect of it instead.  Imagine a clenched fist.  If you are handed something of value, but your hand is metaphorically closed in a fist so to speak, how can you receive it? Can you hold anything with a clenched fist without opening it first? Now imagine that unforgiveness overlays your life like a clenched fist. What can you receive in your life then?

Unforgiveness emanates an energy. It can work against you without you realizing it, sort of opposing you. How do you embrace a clenched fist? You can't leave unforgiveness at home when you choose to and go out without it. It goes where you go. When one holds onto unforgiveness, the negativity of it can be absorbed into one's body on a cellular level, where in time it can become an illness. Unforgiveness can alter one's thoughts. It can mean that what you feel you deserve can seem out of reach. Why? Because unforgiveness takes up space internally that might be better used for what you need and want.

Forgiving others can set you free and allow you to be ... well ... more of you, unencumbered. Fields of study in health, science, and the spiritual have all found a connection between what we think and feel. I.e. what we think translates to what we feel, translates to physical and emotional health, peace of mind or not, and satisfaction or not.

Perhaps we can go so far as to say unforgiveness could be a roadblock to overall prosperity. Once you become aware of this, you can choose to stay locked up with unforgiveness or you can open that door and move forward. I say "locked up" because when one doesn't forgive, it imprisons you in a way. It binds you to that person or circumstance that caused pain or trauma. It locks you up with the negative experience that occurred, which replays in some fashion like an echo. There is no open hand to receive anything new.

Unforgiveness can affect relationships, playing a part in how one does or doesn't relate to others. If it is yourself you need to forgive, that can cause not trusting yourself. Not trusting one's self, which is common with empaths to begin with, can invade many areas of life, including: love, friendships, intuition, and making decisions. When not trusting one's self or others, one may develop assumptions or misinterpretations about others and one's self. This can unconsciously domino onto everyone one interacts with in misinterpreting others with an overlay of past situations. It can distance us from others.

**Forgiveness Saved My Life**

Forgiveness in my life was a huge turning point and I believe it saved my life. Now I have a clean slate, but it wasn't always so. As mentioned previously in this book, I experienced a life and death illness and was on medical leave from work for months. Though I was in treatment with a well-known alternative doctor and two traditional doctors, every day was as severe as the previous day, with no improvement.

After months of weight loss, looking gray like at death's door, I bought the book, "The Prospering Power of Love," by Catherine Ponder, a book of affirmations. What I read stopped me in my tracks, something to the effect of:

> **If you are ill and not healing quickly enough, maybe you need to forgive someone.**

How can that be, I thought. It sounded nonsensical and simplistic. In spite of my doubt, I followed the above thread of thought.

Science says we can change a habit in 3 months. How we think and feel can be perceived as a habit.

In the aforementioned book by Catherine Ponder, I found a Forgiveness Affirmation and began to use it. Using the affirmation, you can replace the negative that binds you to a trauma, person, or situation, with letting go and moving forward. Later I would offer this affirmation to clients in my coaching practice for reprogramming their brain and psyche for a re-set.

So while I was facing life and death, I began the Forgiveness Affirmation. I did it nightly before sleep. After 3 months of no improvement in my severe illness, you can imagine how incredibly surprised I was that after just 2 weeks of starting the affirmation I was seeing my health improve rapidly. Also during that time I read the book, Healing With The Angels, by Doreen Virtue, which I recommend.

The forgiveness affirmation is noted later in this chapter, as well as how to do it and how to know when you've completed forgiveness.

Unforgiveness is like muddy water. Picture your mind, body, and spirit full with mud and ask yourself how that will affect your life. If one is not clear-minded, but instead clouded, can it create decisions that are also metaphorically muddied or cause self-doubt or guilt that gets one stuck?

There may be a number of situations or people to forgive, whether recent or in childhood. You may think that something way back in time doesn't affect you now. If life worked that way it would be great; but it doesn't. Our experiences and memories get tucked away, absorbed into the unconscious. Our cells remember it in the negative until we transform it. It shows up in how one approaches relationships, health, and life in general. These past events become part of one's habits in thinking, feeling, and taking action or not taking action. It affects all outcomes.

There are many different variations regarding forgiveness. You may need to forgive someone or something in your past or present. You may need to forgive someone who died and you felt abandoned, someone who left a love relationship with you, or forgive cruelty at home or in the workplace.

There are many empaths who may have been born into challenging circumstances, and perhaps could not forgive a father or mother for something. It wasn't until later in life I realized the ramifications of unforgiveness affecting my relationships. For instance, if you didn't forgive your father but had a need to, it could affect all relationships you have with men: friendships, work relationships, and intimate relationships. And it can be felt by others in what you resonate; other people can sense something going on there.

There is another facet to this. Unforgiveness might mean one doesn't achieve all they hoped for because unforgiveness imprisons one on the inside. It keeps you attached to the pain of what happened and keeps trauma alive. It stops the healing. You may feel easily triggered, defensive, not open to embrace what may await you. If you become aware that this is living in you, you can work with it. While it might not be like taking a magic pill, and not so pleasant to open up to feeling those emotions again, there are specific steps to get to the other side of it.

## How To Know If You Need To Forgive

When you say an affirmation aloud, if it causes you to suddenly feel a closing of your throat, or tightening of your body in the chest or stomach area, it may tell you that you are carrying an emotional burden related to the matter you're focusing on (even if it occurred a long time ago). This can be a sign you need to forgive someone or something. We can deny it intellectually, but the body takes it on, the body knows. The body is not at ease. Think of the word "dis-ease," disease. Illness can grow in that environment.

So there I was sick in bed with a life and death illness, realizing I had 4 people to forgive. By forgiving each one, I was able to let go of the negative bondage that held back my life and nearly took it from me. Once I completed forgiveness, my whole life changed, literally. It set me free to move forward, and I did.

## Forgiveness & Equilibrium

There may be a number of circumstances or people involved that you feel weigh you down, like a burden you carry. This could be what caused your metaphoric clenched fist, and may cause you to feel defensive. These might be identified by you as areas for forgiveness that close you off from yourself, others, and as mentioned before prosperity. In addition, empaths are very compassionate people, but do not usually offer that compassion to their own self. Instead, most empaths hold themselves responsible for everyone else's burdens which do not belong to them, and emotionally beat themselves up that they should have done more or should have done something differently. This is very common with empaths. Perhaps forgive yourself first for being so hard on yourself.

In forgiving, I don't mean forgetting. We don't want to forget and repeat negative patterns in our life if we can help it. Forgiving can begin the healing process.

Another area where forgiveness may be helpful, is when one is a caretaker for a loved one that is ill or elderly. One may feel caught between a rock and hard place; it can be a tragedy. A very ill or elderly person may have difficulty coping with a loss of control of their body and their life. As a result, they may try to control the lives of others, especially those who caretake them. If they have prolonged pain and strong medication, they may experience a streak of cruelty and lash out. Perhaps learning some new communication skills in this situation might be helpful, especially for empaths who are frequently challenged with boundaries and self-care to begin with. Don't leave yourself behind.

Where anger or guilt occurs, like it may in a caretaking situation, it can be important to release it through forgiveness. In other situations, where anger lingers more than one to two weeks, forgiving can release you from closing yourself off and feeling stuck.

The forgiveness affirmation can be used regarding a work situation. One of my clients worked for a senior person who behaved abusively; everyone at the firm was afraid of him. She made good money and wasn't financially ready to leave her job. Every morning traveling to work by public transportation, she would close her eyes and do the forgiveness affirmation in her head. She would forgive, release, and let go. Each day she was renewed, her clenched fist would open for what life had to offer.

Forgiveness can help you keep your equilibrium. This is something you can do with yourself every day if need be to release any person or situation, clearing your mind, body, and spirit, and free you to distance yourself from negativity. This way it will not take hold of you and you can move ahead in what you need. If you're not able to write the affirmation, you can say it aloud in your car or walking on the street (perhaps have your earbuds attached to a phone, where people think you're engaged in a phone conversation). If you need support, in addition to doing the forgiveness affirmation, there is no shame in that.

Sometimes people prefer to ask God to forgive them. In addition to that, what would it mean to you, if you could forgive yourself, and embrace who you are?

**Forgiveness & Relationships**

I went to an astrologer many years ago, seeking a reading on my love life. I had gone awhile without a love partner, didn't know why, and asked if it was in my chart. He said, "You need to forgive your father. When you do, you will be able to have a lasting love relationship." I was very resistant to what he said, thought it was far-fetched, and felt insulted and emotionally triggered. I know now that emotional triggers are usually a sign there is something valid to pay attention to. This was long before I became ill and learned of the whole forgiveness possibility.

Many years later, I realized just how profound it was what the astrologer told me. After doing the forgiveness affirmation and forgiving my father, it was a game changer. The relationship between me and a man I was later involved with changed radically. I was more open, more accepting, and enjoyed him much more. It was like a door opened and I stepped out of the internal prison. The sense of negative bondage was replaced by harmony and joy. That relationship grew into a 15 year love relationship.

## How To Do A Forgiveness Affirmation

Affirmations are done with repetition, so that they are absorbed into the psyche and become part of who we are. There are two ways you can do an affirmation. I have done it each way and sometimes both ways in the same day.

### (1) Speaking Your Affirmation

When I was very ill, I chose to do the affirmation aloud. I said it aloud one time a night before sleep because it seemed I was more open to receive and absorb it more then, when I was tired and vulnerable. Doing it at night before sleep, one may be less taken up than in the morning when there is a long list of to-dos, or perhaps the need to help your children prepare for their day.

### (2) Writing Your Affirmation

The other way to do your affirmation is to write it 15 times in one sitting. It may seem like it takes longer to absorb when writing, but it is just as effective or more so. It may seem tedious, and as though you're not absorbing it, but you are. I don't recommend typing it; it doesn't work.

You may have a number of people and/or situations you need to forgive. Write a list and prioritize in order of the most pressing on you, i.e. prioritize by the most painful memory and the most damaging to you. You want to release that first. Start with the first item on your list. Work with that one item only, until you know you've completed that forgiveness. Then move on to the next one.

I did otherwise. I worked on forgiving 4 people each night. For some, that may be overwhelming because it can open you to reliving related memories and emotions. I would say the affirmation aloud regarding a particular person. Then I would say it for the next person, and would repeat this process until I said it for each of the 4 people. And would repeat all again the next night.

In writing the affirmation, it could take 30 to 40 minutes per person you're forgiving, with the necessary 15 repetitions. For some, it may take too long to write them each day.

When you say the affirmation aloud and your body tenses or your throat closes, and it's not due to medication, you'll feel the intensity and depth of it, and how much you need to forgive that person or circumstance. For me my throat closed and I could hardly speak the words, it was so painful.

**Forgiveness Affirmation**

"[*insert person's name*], I fully and freely forgive you. I loose and let go. I cast all resentment, judgment, criticism, and unforgiveness unto [*insert divinity you pray to, God, the source, or the universe*] within to be released and healed.

"The prospering truth has set me free to meet my rich good and to share my good with others!"

Repeat this affirmation daily, until you have forgiven.

**How To Know When You've Completed Forgiving**

Of those I've trained on this, they knew when they forgave and released holding onto unforgiveness. Their body felt it, their emotions no longer triggered, and the hurt subsided until it was gone. You'll know. Of the many people I taught this to, one person felt nothing from the beginning, though she thought she needed to forgive. She is not an empath, and there could be a number of reasons for her experience, which would be different than for empaths.

I knew when I spoke the forgiveness affirmation and my throat stopped closing, that I had released that person and circumstance, and was no longer in bondage to the hurt. I was free of it. Of the 4 persons I worked on forgiving, my resolve occurred at different junctures. Some took longer to forgive than others. In forgiveness, I was able to forgive one person in a few weeks, another in 1 month, another in 3 months, and the fourth I don't recall. Give yourself however long it takes. Everyone is different.

**Facebook Post On Forgiveness**

With regard to the most popular and active post I've ever had on my Facebook business page at Corri Coaching, I received an honest comment from a man who shared his thoughts and feelings regarding forgiveness. Below, please find his comment in quotes, followed by my thoughts and then my response.

**Comment On A Facebook Post**

"I have always been able to forgive very quickly and very easily. The problem only truly begins at that moment. I am too quick to forgive and the person feels I'm a sucker and goes straight back and does the original task again. Or because people (including myself) don't expect any realistic attempt at an apology ... both parties say 'I'm good' but nothing can be forgiven or forgotten without being face to face to acknowledge 'hey it's my bad' and 'cool ... that's good enough for me' and the words which signify an agreement is reached, 'Are we good?' 'Oh hell yeah ... of course we're good.' That is a simple but respectful way of apologizing, of forgiving and moving forward without as much as a quick pause in your giddy-up.

"Okay, so I'm sure a lot of people go through this type of thing. People don't expect a realistic attempt at an apology."

## My Thoughts

It appears the man who commented was in a situation where he was trying to be cool and unaffected. But he was affected, and sounded uncomfortable talking about it with the other person. From what he said, my guess is he was uncomfortable because:

(a) he didn't expect a real response;

(b) he sounded uncomfortable to share what he was experiencing, perhaps for fear of rejection or backlash. And ultimately, his approach sidetracked to something other than forgiveness.

Forgiveness is not about expecting anything from anyone else, but rather it's about you and you, and releasing yourself from any negative bondage of a person or situation. Instead, he wanted something else from the other person than the person provided.

## My Response Direct To The Facebook Commenter

The crux of the matter may be in understanding how people around us feel and act. You may be more aware than others. People around you may be acting out, may be unaware of it, and possibly not relating to others. Communication skills are key here. We don't learn them in school. I literally knew nothing about communication skills until I went to coaching school.

However, forgiveness is a more personal experience, solely with one's own self. It's about your relationship with you. It's about what is acceptable to you and what is not. And if something hurts you, do you hold onto that hurt?

If someone repeats a pattern of doing something that affects you personally in an uncomfortable way, it could be that your perception of the situation may be different than theirs. At this point, tweaking communication can be helpful because it can build a bridge between people in understanding, without blaming yourself or the other person.

For example, let's say a group of male friends or people from work are spending time together after work. One of them mocks another in front of everyone, and everyone laughs. It might be helpful to talk to that person in private when no one else is around, whether in person or on the phone. One might express positive things you like about that person, so they know you see them with value. For instance, you like knowing them, you like being around them.

Then you might ask if it's okay to discuss an uncomfortable experience. It's a good idea to ask first, because timing is important. It could be that the other person is not of a clear mind at that moment or may be wrapped up with something else that might throw them off from listening or interacting.

Approaching that conversation could for instance go something like this, "I felt uncomfortable for a short time when we were all hanging out. Is this a good time for me to share it with you?"

This way you are letting the other person know you have a concern that means something to you. You'll notice that it is purposefully not spoken in a playful or joking manner, like: "cool," or "that's my bad." If communicated jokingly or light-heartedly, that's how it will be received. If we don't take ourselves seriously at certain moments, who will? We don't have to point fingers in blame in such a conversation. For example:

"This may be a hot button for me, but when someone says such and such about me in front of others, and others laugh, it doesn't feel good. You know what I mean? Has that ever happened to you?"

Now go slow, and notice the other person's response. Is he honoring what you are saying? Or, is he uninterested? If he's like, "Oh bro, you're too sensitive, man," well then you know he doesn't care how you feel. He'll do it again, it's part of his nature.

We cannot control other people's behavior. In an instance like that, you might ask yourself: How valuable is it to have this person in your life? And what is the cost of it? Does it affect your self-esteem? If there is value for you to know him, or it is a work situation where your colleagues are going out after work together, you might ask yourself: How much time and energy do I want to devote to that? Or, would you prefer to have it be a more peripheral relationship and then fill your personal relationships with more satisfying interactions?

If you decide you want that relationship as is, then it is helpful when you are by yourself to forgive this person using the forgiveness affirmation, to release and let it go. Acknowledge to yourself that he is who he is and you cannot change him. If the other person cannot or will not engage in a conversation about how you are affected by him, then knowing that may change your approach. You can either accept him for who he is, or you can move on. You get to decide.

There are a few other elements to consider. If someone does something repeatedly that you need to forgive them for, you may have a sense of always waiting for the other shoe to drop regarding them, then perhaps you might ask yourself these questions:

(1) What is my part in this?

(2) Am I enabling his behavior?

(3) How can I raise the bar for myself by my behavior, which may rub off on others around me to raise their bar as well?

(4) Do I hold others accountable for what they say and do?

(5) Or do I dismiss their behavior, as though it doesn't mean much, but then it bothers me?

(6) Do I hold myself accountable to what I say I want?

(7) Do I take action to achieve what I say I want?

We teach others how we want to be treated and vice versa. It is a way of building a bridge between people, learning what works for each person, and how to interact going forward. It is part of getting to know another person and their getting to know you.

Learning communication skills is a process that involves understanding the following: one's emotional triggers, clarity on how you feel and what you want, expectations of others, as well as understanding the person you are interacting with and what they feel and want.

*   *   *

When we look at both sides of the fence, we can choose unforgiveness and be attached in bondage, imprisoned to that which pains us. Or we can forgive, let go, and remove the knife in our heart so to speak, allowing healing.

It was after I learned to forgive, that I was able to learn something I never knew I would learn in this life ... unconditional love.

Forgiveness is a great starting place to move forward in all areas of your life.

## Chapter 6 : Follow-Up Items

(1) Assignment:  Forgiveness Affirmation
(2) Reference, Book:  The Prospering Power of Love
(3) Reference, Book:  Healing With the Angels

## (1) **Assignment: Forgiveness Affirmation**

> "[insert person's name], I fully and freely forgive you.  I loose and let go.  I cast all resentment, judgment, criticism, and unforgiveness unto [insert divinity you pray to, God, the source, or the universe] within to be released and healed.
>
> "The prospering truth has set me free to meet my rich good and to share my good with others!"

The above is from the book, The Prospering Power of Love by Catherine Ponder (I may have paraphrased it).

... 1. Write it 15 times a day in one sitting. Typing it doesn't work; it's not absorbed.

... 2. If writing is too tedious, you can print and tape it to the back of your cell phone or some place you will see it, and be able to say it aloud repeatedly throughout the day. Or say it loud before sleep when you are most vulnerable to absorb it.

___
(2) Reference, Book:
**The Prospering Power of Love**, Catherine Ponder

___
(3) Reference, Book:
**Healing With the Angels**, Doreen Virtue

**Chapter 7**

**EMPATHS & LOVE**

We cannot help where we've been and who we've been with. But we can help going forward, where we're going, who we bring into our sacred circle, and who we embrace in love.

For simplicity here, I'm referring to a love interest, a love partner, someone you share intimacy with, i.e. someone who is more than a friend (as opposed to a beloved family member, child, parent, or sibling).

This chapter accommodates single and coupled people. It may provide a new perspective on relationships, giving you a handle in understanding the love you want, and how you will choose to navigate it.

Perhaps you will consider defining for yourself these two things:

(1) What is love?
(2) What do I want from love?

Love can mean different things to different people, yet it is rare that people define and get clear on what they want with love.

In love there are 3 of you. There is you, there is the other person, and there is the unit that makes up the love you share together (it's like a third party). All 3 of these need to be nurtured. It's like a plant. If you don't water and nurture a plant, give it sun, feed it, it's not going to grow, and can wither or die. You are like that plant, as is your partner, and your shared love.

For some, love is a deep connectedness, but for others they may not want deep or connectedness, they haven't done that deep connectedness with their self. For some, love is about unconditional love and acceptance, but that would mean they've already felt that unconditional love and acceptance of their self. For some, it's a financial partnership and companionship, or just one of those. There are other definitions of what love may be. It's best to figure out for yourself what love means to you, and what you want with love.

If you take for granted that your love interest has the same want with love as you do, there could be repercussions. This is a crucial thing in understanding yourself and your love interest. Most people never do this.

We must also take into consideration what our own experience is with self-love. If you've not learned self-love you're not alone, you're in good company. Most people don't know how to do this, including those that have achieved a great deal in their life. Self-love is often something learned by example of what we grew up around and witnessed in every part of our life. It's not taught in school.

The topic of self-love or unconditional self-love can be extra-challenging for empaths, at no fault of one's own. This can be due to feeling misunderstood in childhood and being perceived as too-sensitive, rather than a gifted sensitive. One can develop some self-love with regard to love resonance (see Empath Toolbox, Chapter 2), as well as assignments in the follow-up section at the end of this chapter. Keep in mind unconditional self-love is a learned thing, there is no simple snap your fingers to develop it. I do a private 1-on-1 coaching program to help with self-love and self-esteem building. It involves stripping away what was overlaid onto a person, and replacing it with what the person needs and wants in how they define themselves, to align with one's true and authentic self.

**Earning Love & Respect**

Have you ever considered the idea that love and respect is something we earn and others earn it from us? It took me many years to think this and to realize we can be discerning in love and can select a love partner, as well as our friends. We can select if we want a person that is capable of nurturing and/or capable of being nurtured. Not everyone is capable of nurturing. Years ago, I did not have nurturing in me and was not discerning either. Nurturance might not be important to you. But if it is, then learning what someone is capable of might be helpful to know in terms of a long-range and satisfying relationship. Not everyone is capable of compassion as well, or interested in it. What would it be like for you if compassion is important to you, but after already being involved and invested with a love partner you learn it is not important to them and not part of their emotional skill set?

Did you know most people enter love relationships haphazardly, spontaneously, in a blindfolded sort of way? It's frequently about sexual attraction, and sometimes unconscious attraction to similar patterns experienced in growing up that are familiar. Most people are not careful about who they select. They do not get to know the person before they invest an extensive amount of time, energy, and emotion into a relationship. But ask yourself:

**Would you spontaneously invest your money in a car, without researching if the investment would match what you need and that it would be long lasting?**

People look after their cars with respect, but not their heart and soul, and often not their bodies either. This is very common.

Empaths may be blindfolded so to speak, when viewing who they're dating or living with. Why? While most people do this to a certain extent, let's look at empaths and what many have endured. Many have been ignored, mocked, misunderstood, told they're too sensitive, and for decades may have felt marginal in family, school, work, friends, and love.

Why the blindfold? While an empath is a beacon of light that others are drawn to, while one may have many gifts, it's possible one may not yet realize who they really are, and may not yet appreciate their value. Until an empath becomes empowered, it may be hard to take the blindfold off regarding love, what love is, and what one wants. Another possible reason for the blindfold is the clairsentient experience of being taken up with overwhelm in absorbing energies and emotions of others. After one learns to navigate energy, and live in their own emotions, one's perspective may become clearer.

## Setting A Foundation

How you set a foundation when starting a love relationship can make a difference to what kind of relationship you will have, and may save you extra work and grief. If one uses some caution and self-care and allows time for love to grow into intimate love and vice versa, it creates a different foundation perhaps than what one may have learned.

These days people seem to seek instant everything, right? Foods that are precooked, canned, microwaved, instant download movies, instant medication, instant research, instant cash machines, instant email, and texting while in transit. And then there is ... instant, spontaneous love. This is often found to be something other than love. Not always, but often, it is based on illusion of what people think they want, but frequently has nothing to do with the two people. It's like an overlaying blanket of illusion of what you want onto a love interest, and expecting that's what you'll have, with no real basis for it. Been there done that.

If this type of instant, spontaneous relationship built on illusion lasts, which they usually don't, it could put a person at risk for co-dependency. Why? Because with illusion can come projecting onto another what one needs and wants, without consideration of the person and mutual sharing. A co-dependency type of relationship is where one doesn't function as a whole person on one's own. Up the road it can cause greater need that makes thriving as who one really is more difficult, because one needs the other person to complete them and fulfill the illusion they hold. This is common in our culture and usually occurs because one might not yet know:

(1) how to self-nurture,
(2) one's value, or
(3) one's true self.

It is hard to know how many relationships occur purely out of illusion, tolerating the other person, with little genuine care for them. Genuine care requires understanding and appreciating one's love interest, sharing what one needs, consistent communication, and negotiation.   Even if you're with someone for a lifetime, you're still getting to know them, as people are always changing, and life changes as well.

For those couples living in illusion of what they want the other person to be for them, it can become an unspoken expectation. That expectation can cause frustration and disappointment, rather than appreciation of each other. It's possible that a person's love partner of many years, may actually not know what the other person needs or wants.  A couple may go through many years of marriage never seeing each other clearly for who they are, never communicating what they need and want, living in conflict and power struggles, never negotiating.  After a number of years they may grow increasingly resentful of each other, disappointed, unhappy, and may think all relationships are doomed. In coaching, I've learned many people don't  realize they have options, and so they feel stuck and often believe that's just the way life is.

Trusting what you feel and know, i.e. your intuition, can be your guide in life and in love.  This can be really powerful. It's helpful not to ignore or fault yourself for what you feel.

**Illusion**

Empaths have the capacity to see past a lot of illusion because one deeply feels and knows things. And yet, unless one is empowered, an empath may still get caught up in illusion in relationships. Why? Because of the many reasons self-doubt exists for several years (Chapter 3).

One may have felt misunderstood, lonely disconnected to their feelings, and also not knowing their possibilities and greatness. This can cause many empaths to give up working on their self, and want to join forces with another in love, i.e. join forces to not be lonely in the world. Unfortunately, one can sometimes feel even more lonely being in a love relationship that is not compatible or satisfying. Reworking negative self-talk can allow for attracting and simultaneously seeking the love one deserves, whether starting a new relationship or growing a present one.

**The Love We Deserve**

Here's a story of an empath I coached. She made a lot of money, was an international model when younger, gorgeous in her 40's, created successful businesses, a painter, writer, and a fun person. She dated and had lived with wealthy men, some in positions of power. She seemed like she had it all, right? She was unhappy. She wanted to marry but would not marry any of the many men who asked her because they lied to her, cheated with other women, and mocked her in front of other people. She felt like a doll on the shelf. While she had self-doubt to begin with, each relationship added to it.

All her romances led to frustration and despair. In spite of her having profound knowingness as an empath, underneath the self-doubt was self-talk that ran her off-track regarding love and happiness. She came to discover her inner gremlin, the voice in her head, was telling her no one could love her, she was unlovable. It was a leftover from childhood, at no fault of her own. She was previously unaware of that inner gremlin, yet it metaphorically drove all her love relationships, and caused her to settle for whoever picked her. The follow-up section at the end of this chapter lists a book about the inner gremlin. I've not read it.

When young and vulnerable, what one hears and sees is incorporated into the view of self and continues into adulthood as part of an inner voice. Acknowledging if you have a negative inner voice that is overlaid onto you and may not be aligned with who you really are, is an important first step. A negative inner voice can cause a person to work against their self, or try to be someone other than they truly are. This inner voice can be reworked. Affirmations are helpful to realign with one's authentic self. In the follow-up section at the end of this chapter is a Self-Love Affirmation I created, with instructions of how to use it.

I asked this woman who felt unlovable, of all the men she went with in her life, which of them did she pick? She said, none. She never considered that could be an option. In the follow-up section at the end of this chapter is an assignment to help you figure out what is important to you in picking a love interest, and an assignment for couples to figure out what is important to negotiate on and how to do it.

## Sharing-Nurturing Is A Two-Way Street

Did you ever become intimately involved with someone only to learn, after you invested time, care, and emotion, that they were incapable of caring, sharing, or compassion, and that the relationship was mostly about them? Narcissists are covered later in this chapter.

After you've known someone a long time, how does it feel to share something with them that is challenging and important to you, only to learn they're incapable of listening or can't wait for you to finish talking so they can talk about their self. That can be disappointing.

Empaths can be very nurturing, but is it important to you if sharing and nurturing is a two-way street? So check-in with yourself as to what you need and want. Everyone has their own formula of what works for them.

## Partnering In Love

Did you know you can alter your approach in love if you choose? Your clairs and intuition are your inner compass, your guides. In the same way you learn to slow down enough to feel, hear, and see things that contribute to your knowingness, you can also gather information on what you need and want regarding your love interest. It helps to journal what you sense and receive, without censoring yourself.

Regarding love, sometimes people seek the other person to fill an empty or lonely void within, instead of coming from a place of self-love. When we come from a place of self-love, and are less needy, there is more potential to meet a positive love interest. In that mode of being, there is more possibility of receiving and understanding who the new person you meet really is. As an empath, one has the ability to deeply feel and see beneath the surface of those first time best behaviors.

If you are presently in a love relationship, taking a little bit of time alone can help you figure out what you feel about your relationship. Perhaps explore and journal your answers to the following:

- Have you ever considered what brought you two together?
- What did you want from this relationship?
- Is it the same now as when you met?
- Have any basic needs changed for either of you, that would benefit redefining your relationship?
- What would you like to tweak in the relationship, if anything?
- Does your partner know how you view them?
- Do you know how your partner views you?

You can write down these things and see what you feel in the days and weeks that follow, in order to gain clarity and perspective of you and your relationship.

If you have visited Facebook empath groups, you'll find many of them are full with complaints about unfulfilled love relationships. Much of this is a pattern. The good news is, we can alter patterns. Some things to ask yourself regarding unfulfilled love relationships:

(1) Did I pick someone incapable of what I need and want in a love partner?

People do this a lot, i.e. pick someone who doesn't have the qualities they need or want. An assignment at the end of this chapter should help clarify this for you. Something to keep in mind, we cannot change anyone. So if you're picking someone with a prerequisite that you will need to change them in order to be happy with them, which many do, you are setting yourself up for disappointment.

(2)  Am I discerning?

(3)  Do I need to build on or heal something within myself to attract the type of person I want to be with?

(4)  Are the people I attract not right for me?

If 4 above was a yes, then ask yourself the following question:

(5)  Am I not right with me?

This last question may sound trivial, but it's not. It's amazing how working on and resolving something of this nature, can transform everything in one's life.

**Empaths & Narcissists**

This is a big topic with many empaths. It's common to hear of the empath-narcissist love entanglement and the shell-shock many empaths experience as a result.

An empaths' self-doubt, combined with enormous compassion, plays a large role in the empath-narcissist dichotomy. An empath may beat themselves up emotionally for having that self-doubt, but after a relationship with a narcissist, it is further magnified causing many empaths to retreat from people. It feels damaging; healing needs to occur. If an empath repeats this pattern enough times, they may feel all love is doomed for them.

## How Narcissists Gain Entry To Empaths

I do not believe empaths attract narcissists, but rather empaths attract everyone, as we are beacons of light. However, there is a magnet between empaths and narcissists, due to the patterns of each, that cause them to come together. A narcissist never sees you for who you really are. What is the key to a narcissist gaining entry to an empath? In addition to an empath's self-doubt and compassion for others, some or all of the following three things may exist in an empath that begins a relationship with a narcissist. It can cause you to allow them entry to your sacred love space:

> **(1) I didn't feel or see myself.**
> **(2) I didn't know my value.**
> **(3) I didn't have boundaries.**

When an empath has not yet experienced empowerment, known their value or their boundaries, they may seek love in an open and vulnerable way, with no discernment. A type of vulnerability that can be diminishing. We want to be strong like a backbone and vulnerable like an open hand. One without the other does not work for us.

This pattern doesn't exist with just narcissists. Empaths have so much to give, so much great energy, they don't realize that their light can be diminished, their body drained, their soul emptied. So it helps to keep this in mind if you're not sure that a person is right for you yet. Be open-minded and neutral until you know, and of course be kind. Also, it can do an empath well to learn to have balance in give and take, as empaths are often givers, leaving themselves behind.

Have you ever heard of soul murder (see Chapter 4)? This can occur in a damaging childhood, but can also occur in adult life. Perhaps be mindful to preserve yourself in what is best for you. Give your love but don't give away your soul.

Let's look at the profile of both types of people, empaths and narcissists, for clarity in how it all fits together.

**Empaths**

Empaths are usually very devoted in love, very giving, compassionate, energetic, beacons of light. The light we emit draws people to us. One also has a tendency to forget about their self, allows one's self to be eclipsed, unheard, unspoken (see Empaths & Communication, Chapter 8), and empaths often leave their self behind. Narcissists see the empath's love and beacon of light, but they also see the self-doubt and lack of confidence.

**Narcissists**

Narcissists usually seek and demand a deep devotion and a lot of attention. They often behave entitled, manipulative, controlling, unappreciative, demanding, and lack feeling for others. However they can be very sensitive about themselves, it is all about them. In the follow-up section at the end of this chapter is an article regarding four types of narcissists and how they may show up.

Many people think that by loving a narcissist, you can heal and change them, and all will be fine. It doesn't work like that.

There is nothing you can do to change a narcissist. We cannot change anyone, except ourselves.

If an empath were joyful, confident, and empowered, a narcissist may still pursue them, though it's less likely, and I doubt it would last long. An empowered empath would trust what they saw, felt, and heard, without doubt, and would honor their own value. An empowered empath would most likely see a narcissist as trouble and would probably not invite them into their sacred space.

## 11 Ways To Avoid Getting Involved With A Narcissist

### (1) Be cautious about absorbing flattery.

Since narcissists live in an entitlement mode of being and lack feeling for others, how might a narcissist win over a love interest you may ask? It may be done with flattery or flashing something they know an empath needs or wants. Caution with this.

You may want to avoid absorbing flattery from someone who doesn't really know you. Don't let it influence you. Keep in mind it's not about you, but about the illusion a narcissist wants to create. It's all on the surface. It's about what they want to see or what they do to get what they want. You can be polite and neutral regarding flattery.

When somebody really gets to know you, the compliments are real, they see you from the inside out. When we're in our teens, 20's, and 30's, we may love hearing flattery about how we look. When we grow older, we may like flattery about how we look, but also want to be accepted for who we are. If you feel that way in your 20's and 30's, you are ahead of the game. The external in how we look always changes, and sometimes the internal does too.

Empaths can easily be taken in, perhaps by flattery, starving for attention, understanding, and appreciation. But go slow, take time to get to know someone. Allow your clairs and your intuition to help guide you in love.

**(2)  Read a person by their actions, rather than words.**

Some people have a disconnect between what they say and what they do. They may know how to speak with words that spark us, they know what to say, they have heard those words on TV, in a movie, or read them in a book, but it may have little to do with who they are if they have that disconnect. So it's best to pay attention to a person's actions rather than their words.

**(3)  You have great value and importance.**

Remember the great value and gifts you bring to the world, just by being born with all this light and compassion inside you. You can make a list of the Gems of Who You Are and continually add to it. This is an Assignment in the follow-up section at the end of this chapter. You don't need a love partner to flatter you, before you can love who you are. When we value who we are, we tend to attract those that will value us as well. A healthy person is okay with learning to get to know you and being around you.

## (4) Do you know the 5 non-negotiable items that are important to you in a love partner?

Of course one would not share such things with a new date. But as one gets to know a person, has several dates and phone calls, a question here and there can give you insight to those things that are important to you. See Assignment in the follow-up section at the end of this chapter.

## (5) Are they kind to strangers?

A narcissist may be kind to you in the beginning, but pay attention to who they really are when they interact with strangers. Are they kind to strangers?

## (6) Do they act entitled?

If you are with a narcissist that expects the world to revolve around them, they'll likely expect the same from you. After the initial glow and excitement of a new relationship and the preliminary attention that a narcissist showers on you to win you over, being with a narcissist can be very lonely.

## (7) Do they nurture their own self?

If they're unable to nurture their own self, how can they nurture a relationship? Just as plants need water and sun to grow, relationships need care to grow.

## (8) Are they kind when they talk about their friends?

Listening to them talk about their friends can offer insight as to how they feel about the people closest to them, both men and women. Paying attention can help you learn a lot about their capacity to relate to and care for those in their life.

## (9) Are they all about image?

Is there any substance to what they represent and what is important to them or is all about image and how they want to appear to others?

## (10) What are their top values and priorities?

Are you able to learn of their values and priorities? As you spend more time with them, do they reveal more of themselves, or are they secretive?

## (11) Do they complain a lot about people or circumstances?

If a narcissist is sharing a lot of complaints with you about people and circumstances, up the road they will likely complain about you to others. Such a person is not looking for solutions or the cup half full, but rather half-empty. Their focus may be on problems. It's possible such a person will see a love relationship as a problem.

Empaths tend to take on the role of fixer-rescuer of everyone except themselves (Chapter 2), leaving their self behind, feeling resentful, uncared for, and treated badly. This is where an empath gives up their power, unless trained to help other people and there is energetic exchange. When an empath can avoid trying to rescue others, that energy and focus can be used for self-growth and developing empowerment.

How does an empath alter the pattern of rescuing others, or giving up their power and soul to a narcissist, instead of rescuing their own self? We always want to respect another person's soul path and what they came here to do, whatever that is (Chapter 4). It is not up to us to fulfill that for someone else. One can alter the rescuer pattern by building self-esteem, self-worth, becoming more aware of what one wants, and allowing feeling one's own emotions, rather than focusing only on the emotions of others. These things will help you to no longer be drawn to narcissists. Narcissists are not attracted to functional, healthy empaths, at least not for long. Empowered empaths can see right through them, and can steer clear.

*     *     *

You can teach others in a kind way how you want to be treated. This allows them to connect with you and get to know you in a deeper way, as well as create boundaries. You might be surprised how many people appreciate this in any type of relationship. It can also be accomplished in preexisting relationships. Have coached some in 20 year marriages that brought in new boundaries of how they wanted to be treated and it improved their love relationships, as well as other relationships.

There may be certain absolutes for each person. If you tell someone what is important to you, and they cross the line of your boundaries repeatedly, then perhaps they are unable to accept who you are and how you feel. Even if a person doesn't totally understand how you think and feel, they can still respect boundaries and honor you and vice versa. Do you want to be with someone who is okay running roughshod over you? But first and foremost, embracing who you are will allow you to embrace another and them you. Otherwise, the relationship may not be a growing relationship, could accumulate problems, and may in the long run feel more like an acquaintance rather than a supportive love partner.

Because we cannot change or fix another person, and loving a person cannot heal or change them, any change or healing in a person must initiate from the person their self. To hope to change someone else can cause not only unrequited love and stress, but can affect one's health. If a love interest wants to resolve their life and seek help, one can be supportive, but trying to be their rescuer gets in the way of their soul path, as well as one's own soul path, and can create a double-whammy for an empath. It can cause an empath to absorb that person's emotions, needs, and wants, and to lose track of their own self.

*     *     *

When an empath has healthy boundaries, gives and receives equally in understanding and love, when it is with another healthy, energetic soul, it need not diminish your light or energy, but can increase it.

A healthy love relationship starts first from within. As an empath builds their self up, a more equal, caring, and energetic exchange in love can come into play.

## Chapter 7 : Follow-Up Items

(1) Assignment #1:  Single People: 10 Qualities You Want in A Love Partner & 5 Non-Negotiables
(2) Assignment #2:  Existing Couples – Assignment #1 and

Exploring & Negotiating
(3) Assignment #3: Affirmation, Self-Love
(4) Assignment #4: Exercise, Unconditional Self-Love
(5) Reference, Article: Empaths Attract 4 Types Of Narcissists
(6) Reference, Book: Taming Your Inner Gremlin

_____
## (1) **Assignment #1: Single People: 10 Qualities You Want In A Love Partner & 5 Non-Negotiables**

This assignment is to learn what love means to you, and the qualities you want in a love relationship.

Instructions
... 1. First figure out what "love" means to you. Perhaps write it down in your journal.

... 2. Make a list of 10 qualities you would like a love partner to have.

... 3. Out of the 10 qualities above, pick 5 that are non-negotiable for you, meaning that it's very important to you that this person has those 5 qualities.

... 4. Put those 5 qualities in order of priority from the most important as number 1 and put them in order to the 5th.

... 5. If you are single, figure out where you would go to meet someone with the first 5 qualities.

... 6. Meditate on meeting a love interest. Ask for information like: Where is this person you want to meet?

And pay attention to what you receive in the days, weeks, months to come.  See if you can put together a list of places.

... 7.  In meditation, ask:  What does this person look like?  And pay attention to what you receive in the days, weeks, months to come.

... 8.  Ask divinity in mediation:  Is this person looking for you already?  See if you receive any information in days, weeks, months to come.  Pay attention to how you receive information with your clairs.  Every empath is different in how soon and what way information comes to them.

_____

## (2) **Assignment #2:  Couples -- Assignment #1 and Exploring & Negotiating**

Instructions:
... 1.  Do steps 1-4 above in Assignment #1.

... 2.  Ask your love partner if he-she will try this exercise, doing steps 1-4.  They write it privately on their own.

... 3.  Then share your lists together.  Did anything match up?

... 4.  If you have different non-negotiables in their first 5 qualities, ask your partner if they can be negotiated.

... 5.  How do you feel about the two lists, yours and your partner's?  Write in your journal what you feel so you can allow your feelings to emerge.  See if you can accept your feelings and embrace them.

... 6. Are you willing to discuss your non-negotiables with your love partner?

... 7. How do you feel about your love partner's response regarding non-negotiables? Are they willing to discuss it?

... 8. Did you learn anything about your present relationship?

... 9. Is there room for growth?

.. 10. How does this Assignment make you feel?

_____
## (3) Assignment #3: Affirmation, Self-Love

Instructions:
Tweak the below Affirmation to make it yours.
Write or say it aloud, daily.

... 1. Write it 15 times a day in one sitting. Typing it doesn't work, it's not absorbed.

... 2. If writing is too tedious, you can print and tape it to the back of your cell phone or some place you will see it, and be able to say it aloud repeatedly throughout the day. Or say it aloud before sleep when you are most vulnerable to absorb it.

... 3. An affirmation not only sets your intention but is absorbed into your psyche, your very being. Repeat it daily until you absorb it.

... 4. Once you've absorbed it, take note if there is a difference in how you feel and your outcomes. Some affirmations are absorbed in weeks, some in several months. Everyone is different.

... 5.  Affirmations put us back into alignment with who we really are and in our metaphoric driver's seat.  It reprograms the brain and gives us a re-set.

> I love myself unconditionally.
> I have compassion for whatever I have endured.
> I am love.
> And all is well.

## (4) **Assignment #4:  Exercise, Unconditional Self-Love**

Instructions:

... 1.  This a small beginning in approaching self-love, but a beginning nonetheless.

... 2.   In front of the mirror tell yourself:

> "I love you [*insert your name*]."

At first it may feel awkward and uncomfortable.  Do it as often as you can, until it doesn't feel awkward anymore.

... 3.  When you are more comfortable with this assignment, then every time you have a bad day - or someone has a go at you that might feel harsh, say aloud to yourself:

> "I love you [*insert your name*].  You're doing a great job!"

146

... 4. Does this assignment lessen some of the harshness? Does it makes you feel better about yourself, maybe more supported?

... 5. Did you ever become enamored in love with someone?

How did that make you feel?  For a time did it make you feel like you had a special place in the world?  You belonged? Alive?

That is what unconditional self-love can feel like.

_____
(5)  Reference, Article: **Empaths Attract 4 Types Of Narcissists**, David Wolfe
https://www.davidwolfe.com/empaths-attract-4-types-of-narcissists/

_____
(6)  Reference, Book:  **Taming Your Inner Gremlin: A Surprisingly Simple Method for Getting Out of Your Own Way**, Rick Carson

# Chapter 8

## EMPATHS & COMMUNICATION

### Compromised Communication

Many empaths have experienced large segments of their life where they felt unheard, ignored, and marginalized. You're gifted in beautiful ways and are more powerful than you may know.

My grandmother told me this story. As a very young child, barely able to walk, my mother was concerned I may be retarded. She didn't think I behaved as most children, and I did not speak at the same age the way my older brother did. My mother could not understand my speech or manner but my brother understood and would interpret. She brought me to a doctor to be diagnosed. The doctor handed me a lollipop in a wrapper. My mother told him he shouldn't give that to me as I've never seen one, wouldn't know what to do with it, and could hurt myself. I took the wrapper off and put the lollipop in my mouth, holding the stick. He told my mother that I was advanced for my age, and jokingly told her she was retarded.

Some empaths at a young age may have felt excluded, not supported and embraced by family, school, and friends. At age 5 my mother said she was afraid of me because she claimed I could see inside her and know things about her. Can this lack of support and being marginalized affect communication? You bet it can! How? Some empaths may lose touch with their inner and outer voice. They may become silent, in a bubble of sorts, feeling isolated. Once provided tools, I see empaths make major and rapid shifts in their lives, quicker than most other people.

Listed below are some ways challenges endured by empaths may show up in their communication. These are generalizations, of course, not specific to all, and may vary by degree.

## (1) Silent vs. Shy

Many empaths say they are shy or don't talk much because it is their nature or personality.

### Definition Of Shy

> "being reserved or having or showing nervousness or timidity in the company of other people"

With empaths, being shy is not necessarily a personality trait that belongs to them by nature, but one that is a side effect of what they have endured. It can be a lack of confidence and self-esteem, fear of retribution of being judged or mocked, and overall it may be a consequence of feeling unaccepted. Empaths may live in a victim mode, experiencing a high level of self-blame. This appears to be common with empaths and is one that can be processed through to the other side of it. One may not be used to being heard, which can be painful, and so one gets used to being silent and may, on the face of it, appear shy.

## Solution: Acknowledge, Validate,
##            Know Your Worth, Find Your Voice

This is a great order of events in finding one's voice. Acknowledging and validating who you are, and how you arrived at this place in your life, creates an understanding that can lessen the burden of self-blame one may carry. It's extremely important for empaths, like anyone else, to know your worth, value, and importance. It is crucial not to wait for others to acknowledge and validate you, but as you can, to do that for yourself.

Something that helps in self-training in communication, is slowing down, measuring your words, and considering using less words in order to hold more weight in speaking concisely. This can in a humble way allow your power to emerge in speaking.

Empaths have strong intuition and often knowing, but I would caution imparting knowledge to someone who is not seeking that from you, as it can cost you a relationship. Interaction, communication, is a dance. Ask yourself, "Is the dance occurring with all involved, or is it one-sided." You want to make room for others that might not be as swift as you in their knowingness, as they may not have the same gifts you have, but also make sure there is room for you as well in the conversation.

## (2) Rapid Speech

If at an early age one is repeatedly cut off when speaking, turned away, mocked, or ignored, one may grow up feeling what they think or say is not important. This may cause a person to speak rapidly to fit in a lot of information, before

150

being cut off.  Unfortunately, when speaking quickly, others may tend to tune out.

**Solution:  Learn To Slow Down Your Speech**

If one meditates daily, it can in time naturally alter speech to a more even pace, which is easier for others to listen to. Once your speech slows down, it may then be difficult for you to listen to a rapid speaker.  It may feel draining or hard to follow for you.

You could try practicing speaking aloud when home alone. See if you can slow it down and give more merit to the words you say.  You can try journaling what you'd like to say, or type it, and edit it as many times as you need, to make it clear and concise.  Then try reading it aloud again, slowly.

## (3) Rambling

Because empaths may go through stretches of time not being heard, spending much time alone, or spending time hearing others and helping others, they may have lost their own voice.

Rambling occurs when one goes on and on inserting various details that may have little or nothing to do with the conversation at hand.  It can be like the floodgates open and so much spills out.  It is as though one is making up for lost time in speaking. It is more 1-sided in speech than a interactive conversation, those that hear this rambling may get lost in the details, and lose track of what is being said or what the point of it is.

For a great many years, I rambled in 1-sided speech with others. I was unaware of doing this and only learned of it when a man I was involved with did the following. He would:

(1) interrupt me and ask me to get to the point,
(2) snored, or
(3) told me how painful it was to listen to me.

His honest response was beyond valuable. It caused me to retrain my speech patterns. I only point out myself in this, so you can know I had some issues in communication that was resolvable. I have coached a number of empaths that experienced this as well. Together, we retrained their communication skills to what they wanted, and it helped alter their outcomes. You can tweak your communication process if you choose to.

When we ramble, others may sense we are out of synch with our self. For instance, it may appear one is insecure, needy, don't think much of one's self, or can't think clearly. Others may view a rambler as weak.

Let's break down some of the reasons an empath may ramble and some solutions. Rambling can be driven by triggered emotions, but can also be a habit leftover from the past.

... **1. Pain** – One may ramble trying to veil inner emotional pain.

... **2. Control** – One may feel their life is out of control. This may cause one to want to control their environment, including conversations. Keep in mind, many empaths are absorbing energy and emotions of others around them, even at a distance. This can feel quite out of control.

... **3. Directing** – If one feels they have been marginalized as an empath a good deal of their life and not heard, they may feel a push to direct conversations, which seem like controlling, but really it may represent a need to direct one's internal self-talk.

## Solution

While solutions for this might be very individualized, there are a few things that can be attempted. Just like anything else, trying things to see what works best for you is the ticket.

Regarding soul repair and soul healing, see Chapter 4. Regarding emotional pain and healing, see Chapter 5.

Some steps you can take:

(1)   In partnering with divinity, you can write a letter to divinity to ask for healing in anything and also ask for solutions. Then light a candle in a glass jar regarding same and place the letter under the candle.

(2)  You can journal, so your higher self can take you to your next right step.

(3)   Meditation can help you to receive information on healing solutions provided by your higher self, divinity, and spirit guides.

(4) You can try affirmations to reprogram your self-talk. You can also use self-help books to learn to reconnect to your authentic self in new ways, then learn to reconnect to others and the world at large.

While the following is not a 100% complete solution for rambling, these two things can make a difference in first steps.

... **1. Meditation.** This helps empaths gain clarity and focus on their thoughts. In time, it may create peace and calm. Then practice two-way conversations where your comments can be shortened and interactive.

... **2. Journaling.** This can help to collect one's thoughts. It's also a form of purging to release the sludge that is taking up space in thought and emotion. It is like speaking to the universe in writing. It too may help clarity and focus.

Go easy and give yourself time to adapt to trying new communication skills. Don't beat yourself up about it. Try being patient with yourself, give yourself a hug, and reward yourself for each step tried.

... **3. Practice Being Concise.** Rambling may also occur in writing, in emails. If you find yourself doing this, you can train yourself by editing and reducing everything to its most concise and clearest form, with the least amount of words. It may take time to get used to, and that's okay. Eventually it will become your way of being.

... **4. The Void Or Emptiness.** Rambling can occur, alongside unconsciously shutting off emotional pain. It's usually due to something unresolved within, so it may become like a void space within, without feeling, or can be a feeling of emptiness. This is where an empath after years of trying to shut off absorbing others' emotions, may have lost touch with their own. It may be difficult identifying what one feels about something in their own life. And so making a decision about it, can be challenging.

There are times one may feel they need to disconnect from what they feel and know, in order to function in daily life. It can, though, cause blocking abundance, satisfaction, and joy. It is best to reach out to someone trained that can help, or find a local support group where you can reconnect to your emotions.

... **5. Brain Chatter.** Many empaths experience brain chatter. It may be due to excess stress in multiple areas of life. It could also be from childhood, if one experienced oppression or repression. One's brain may focus on things in the past that float up and overlay onto the present. With brain chatter, one may feel the need to explain things over and above, to validate that what one is thinking, feeling, or saying, has meaning, worth, and that it makes sense to others. Or it could be to override self-blame, shame, or guilt. This is common with empaths, and resolvable.

## Solution

One can meditate and still have brain chatter, though it may lessen. Usually, it is best for a person to explore where their stress comes from, how it shows up, what they perceive, and what is their approach and process in thought, emotion, and actions. Does one need healing and resolve about something in the past that is working on them? How much of one's stress is due to external circumstances? And how much of one's stress is due to internal circumstances (i.e. thoughts and emotions) and/or blocks, such as: limited beliefs, misinterpretations, assumptions, or an inner gremlin voice that talks one down. Thought's can be reprogrammed; it's like a re-set. An experienced Certified Professional Coach can assist with this.

... **6. Complaining.**    Complaining is the opposite of gratitude.  It can be a result of:

(1)  feeling powerless;
(2)  a habit through osmosis growing up,
(3)  a victim mode of being to garner care from others.

By complaining one may get attention or get others to support them, which may feel like love, taking the place of self-love.

There are those that approach everything in life in a complaint mode of being, in thought and speech.  Gossip is prevalent in our culture, and is a form of complaint, complaint about others.  I do wonder if someone gossips a lot, do they experience a lot of complaining thoughts about their own life and the world at large.  Complaining takes one off course and is consuming. It will take the place of productivity, achievement, and satisfaction.  Often people complain when they feel unable to create the life they want, or are unable to feel the way they want.

Complaining can become very engrained and a hard habit to break.  For some it may be like purging the inner sludge or purging the feeling of being put down, but unfortunately, complaints create more complaints, and moves a person further into living in lack, as opposed to gratitude and manifesting what one wants.

**Solution**

The great thing is that just as one learns to adopt a habit, one can learn to break it.

**Complaint Journal**

Start a Complaint Journal. Have it be a size that can easily go with you wherever you go. Fill it only with complaints.

Every time you have a complaining thought or say something that sounds like a complaint, write it in your Complaint Journal. If you are with someone in a restaurant, you can excuse yourself, go to the wash room, and write it down. Keep your Complaint Journal going until you no longer have any complaints left to write down, however long that takes, even if it's a year or longer.

People that are complainers might even have no idea how many complaining thoughts they have in a day, or even in an hour. The Complaint Journal helps you get an idea of how you are operating in this way. It helps to know that if you are thinking numerous complaints on a regular basis, it will influence the outcomes in your life.

Thoughts = Emotions = Actions = Outcomes

Change your thoughts, change your outcomes.

... **7. Feeling Diminished In Communication**.     If you feel diminished in communication, are unsure of yourself when speaking to strangers, are uncomfortable perhaps with those you know, whether close people in your life or in business, journaling and meditating for focus and clarity might help somewhat.

## Solution

Feeling diminished, you might best benefit by doing a Personal Development Program with a Certified Professional Coach. You can take an assessment, get a reading on the assessment, and plan a course of action, using workbooks together with a coach. This has proved quite valuable for my clients in building self-esteem, communication skills, and emotional intelligence. My clients have been thrilled with the transformation they experienced, with results they never imagined were possible.

Also important is that others know you have a backbone and you will speak up for yourself. Ask for what you want, you just might get it. And you deserve it. But also stand up for yourself.

Some empaths, because they doubt themselves, may step back into the shadows, and avoid communication where possible. Because empaths are so loving, and full with compassion for others, people may misinterpret their friendliness as a sign of weakness or as a pushover. Getting stronger in one's self, learning to release stress, asking for what you want, and not allowing anyone to push against what you need and want, can take practice. As one's communication gets stronger and empaths speak up for themselves, shortly thereafter it won't be necessary to do that much. You can be appreciated for who you are. Setting boundaries can help others to get to know you (see Chapter 10).

If you have a habit of putting yourself down and belittling yourself in front of others, as most empaths tend to do, from this day forward see if you can catch yourself and avoid doing this. It can be healthy to laugh at one's self and not take one's self seriously all the time, but that's not what I'm talking about. I'm referring to your getting used to the value of you. Show others by example that you value yourself, and others will learn to do the same. We teach others how we want to be treated. If someone belittles you, let them know that's not what you're about, and that's it's not acceptable. If they are close to you, they might apologize.

**From this day forward, assure yourself you have something important to say and you're going to say it.**

One can still be discerning. That is, you don't need to share your clairs and gifts with those that are not in your sacred circle, if it will only create conflict for you. Tell yourself that from this day forward you will honor what you feel and will speak up for what you want with family and friends. Continuing to write in your journal can assist you in finding your voice.

If your inner voice is talking you down and getting in your way, see Chapter 7 regarding the inner gremlin.

---

**Chapter 8 : Follow-Up Items**

(1) Assignment: Affirmation For Finding Your Voice
(2) Reference, Book: Taming Your Inner Gremlin

----

## (1) Assignment: Affirmation For Finding Your Voice

Tweak this affirmation to make it your own.

> I am strong.
> I am good.
> I am who I am supposed to be.
> I think as I should.
> What I have to say is important.
> And I'm going to say it.

... 1. Write it 15 times a day in one sitting. Typing it doesn't work; it's not absorbed.

... 2. If writing is too tedious, you can print and tape it to the back of your cell phone or some place you will see it, and be able to say it aloud repeatedly throughout the day. Or say it aloud before sleep when you are most vulnerable to absorb it.

... 3. In time, take note: Is it causing you to speak up for yourself? Are others starting to take notice and listening?

----

(2) Reference, Book: **Taming Your Inner Gremlin: A Surprisingly Simple Method for Getting Out of Your Own Way**, Rick Carson

## Chapter 9

## INTUITION: YOUR INNER COMPASS

Our intuition is a great part of our inner compass, our inner guidance system as empaths. If you get clear with your intuition, you will be able to better guide the direction of your life. It's a big part of how we relate to the world. If your intuition is shut off, you may be missing out on possibilities in connecting to yourself, others, and life in general.

In such a busy world, with so many responsibilities, until one learns the Empath Toolbox to navigate energy to live in one's own energy and emotions, some empaths may shut down their intuition to get by. There is so much to wrap your head around, it's understandable.

Learning the Empath Toolbox (Chapter 2), selecting the tools that work for you, and having others' energies become peripheral like background noise is a high priority for empaths. Then it is helpful to learn more about your empath gifts (Chapter 3), which clairs and additional empath gifts are activated in you, how to recognize them, and how to use them. After empaths in learn what is covered in Chapters 2 and 3 herein, there is usually a marked increase in confidence and decrease in the curse of being an empath. Thereafter, exploring one's intuition becomes more inviting. Perhaps you are ready now to reawaken to your intuition, if you haven't already. It is one of your natural superpowers

As empaths, we are born with heightened abilities in intuition. You may already be self-assured and trusting in what you receive. But for those that are not yet sure of their intuition, or it's shut down, self-trust is primary to opening that door. And so this chapter explores the many things that may get in the way of an empath and their self-trust. Later in this chapter we get into one's Body Compass as a tool for intuition. Sometimes awareness and clear focus on such, promotes forward movement.

## Self-Trust vs. Self-Doubt

- How does self-trust show up in your life? Or does it?
- What can self-trust mean to your life?
- When was the last time you took a leap of faith with something?
- Did you know beforehand what the outcome would be, without any rational reason for knowing it?

The above questions and more come into play where self-trust and leap of faith is concerned. Also involved are assumptions and misinterpretations, which are blocks that can stop self-trust, because of something that happened in the past that didn't go well. One may feel it will inevitably happen again. This type of thinking creates anxiety and fear, though an assumption might not be true in present or future circumstances. This is very common.

Sometimes shutting down intuition, due to past challenges, can create caution with reason. Practicality and reason is of great use. Intuition, however, is a whole other ball of wax, where one can utilize knowledge and understanding, without reason, you just do. As an empath, you have great options for accessing your intuition, especially if you practice meditation. Regular meditation helps eliminate anxiety and doubt. In addition, Partnering With Divinity and Your Spirit Guides (Chapter 5) may add a sense of support.

Let's explore the many ways self-trust can come be of great help. Perhaps you will journal how you feel regarding each of the below items.

## (1) Using Your Clairs To Access Information

One of an empath's greatest assets is picking up energy and emotions of others in mind, body, and spirit. Let's say you meet someone for the first time, whether in person or online. You sense something about this person in the positive or negative. Your gut feeling tells you to approach someone or avoid someone. Do you listen to it? See the Assignment Reading People Energetically, in the follow-up section at the end of this chapter.

## (2) What You Want v. What You Know

When I was younger, I did not listen to what I knew intuitively, i.e., what my inner compass told me. In my journal I'd write what I felt about a new friend, teacher, or boyfriend. And then I would forget about it, bypassing what I wrote. There are different reasons for this regarding self-doubt (Chapter 3).

Another reason for bypassing what one knows from the start may have to do with wanting so much to have a new friend, new teacher, or new boyfriend, that one avoids what they sense. You may want to move ahead on that new relationship and override your knowing and clairsentience, due to feeling alone or lonely, and you ignore what you know.

## (3) Conditioning & Disconnect

When a child repeatedly witnesses a parent that does not mean what they say, or that what they say does not match their actions, there can be a disconnect. The disconnect may be in the parent, but children tend to mirror and absorb what is around them, and often it becomes part of who they are. Growing up in such an environment, later as an adult one might question their self because one does not trust what they feel, hear, and see. As a result, these thoughts may occur:

- Is what I think is happening, really happening?
- Is this really what is true?
- Is this really what I feel?

Perhaps journaling on these things can help you understand more about yourself with this. It took me many years to bridge that gap, the disconnect between what a parent says and what they do, and questioning myself as an adult. It took inner work before I trusted what I thought and felt, before I was able to accept what I knew instantaneously, and could stop questioning myself on everything. This could spill onto how one hears and views other people in their life as well. You may think:

- Is that person really saying what they mean?
- Can I trust that this person will do what they say?

Because we are frequently drawn to the familiar, i.e. to character traits of a parent, until we learn more about our own authentic self, this experience may be compounded by choosing a love partner that also says one thing and does another.

When younger, while I doubted and mistrusted myself, at the same time I trusted everyone else, excessively, without any discernment. Trust of others at that time, had nothing to do with intuition or rationale, but rather related to how I trusted my parent whose words did not match their actions. I.e., I trusted my parent and mistrusted myself. In that vein, I would give away all my trust to others and would leave myself behind. So check-in with yourself if you have self-doubt, and ask yourself:

**Are you haphazardly giving all your trust to others, but not trusting yourself?**

This is very common with empaths. I repeat this sentence a lot through the book, as there are themes that have affected most of us. If you are doing this, then learning to have unconditional self-love (Chapter 7), self-nurturance, and perhaps giving yourself six months to a year of self-growth, might go a long way to assist you.

Intuition involves learning what is going on with one's self, without judging.

## (4) Allowing Intuition Outside The Box

- Do you allow yourself to feel what you feel?
- Did you know many people don't "allow" their self this, whether empaths or not, and often censor their own self as to what they feel?

An attorney I used to coach told me in session he wasn't allowed to think for himself as a child and still as a adult. While he worked for a large corporate firm, he was challenged in allowing himself to think outside the box and it affected his communication, both at work and at home. You may think this is odd for an attorney in a profession that is all about perception and communication, but when it is about one's own life and personal thoughts and feelings, this is more common than you know.

He recalled that in school at age 7, when he would contribute or ask for help with anything, the teacher would always say: "Go sit down," or would suggest he be quiet. This was reinforced at home as well. As an adult, he didn't realize this "go sit down" theme lived in him. It was ruling him from the inside out, stopping him from embracing any new thought of his own, only accepting what was found in a book. As a result, he did not know what he felt about most things. It was like a closed door to his feelings. In time, with practice, in dissecting thoughts on a regular basis, with patience, and asking the following questions, he was able to access his feelings.

- Is this true for you?
- If not, what else could it be?

So ask yourself, do you allow what you think to be true or of substance?

## (5) Past Experience & Assumptions

If one had past experiences that were disappointing and unresolved, it may cause a cloud over one's head so to speak, and challenge making decisions. When young, if one did not witness parents or been in a learning environment where there was clear, focused communication, and decisions were made of benefit, one may not yet have a handle on turning mistakes or twists in the road into positive outcomes. At times of making decisions, one may instead question or judge their self.

Did you ever make a decision in the past that didn't work out well? I knew someone from school who started three businesses, all of which, in his view, failed. As a result, for several years thereafter he avoided moving forward in business.

What if you could view your past decisions and outcomes as life lessons? Could you learn anything from it? Could something that didn't go well, still be viewed as a gift (Chapter 4). Is it possible it brought you to something more meaningful or valuable that you might have missed otherwise?

Are you making assumptions, as many people do, that because you were wrong about sensing or trying something, that you will be wrong again and so you doubt yourself? This is where journaling can help to keep you on track of where you're at, how well you are doing with what you sense and know, how much you can trust yourself or not, and your self-talk if talking yourself down.

Did you know Thomas Edison's teachers said he was "too stupid to learn anything"? He was fired from his first two jobs for being nonproductive. As an inventor, he made 1,000 attempts at inventing the light bulb. Does that mean the first 999 times "failed"? Our culture designates success in very black and white terms as though you're either successful or you're not. But success rarely moves in a straight line, and has many gray areas. Perhaps if we can replace the word failed, to instead be that: Thomas Edison's **mistakes were his stepping stones to success**. If he had chosen to look at his past mistakes as a failures, making an assumption that what occurred in the past would be the same going forward, he might have given up. Without those mistakes, he would not have arrived at the light bulb that we all take for granted today. We light up our nights, thanks to Thomas Edison and his many attempts.

## (6) Interference

There are times in all of our lives we may feel railroaded and off-track, internally, externally, or both. When in the middle of a major challenge, it can interfere with one's natural flow and perspective. It can cause questioning one's self. "Everything was going so well, now this. What did I do wrong?" There are some times when going off-track may last longer than other times.

How much compassion do you feel for yourself at such a time? Most empaths have so much compassion and love for others, and little or none for their self. Every time you run up against a challenge that stops you from accessing your self-trust, or maybe you have not felt much self-trust yet, and while I repeat myself yet again, there are two things to consider that are so pertinent to intuition.

... 1. Learning self-love, self-nurturance, can allow you to embrace yourself in new ways that may feel odd at first, but can be very rewarding. In the follow-up section at the end of Chapter 7, see Assignment #3: Self-Love Affirmation and Assignment #4: Exercise for Unconditional Self-Love.

... 2. If you did not grow up with love around you, as many empaths did not, sometimes one needs soul healing (see Chapter 4). In these circumstances, self-trust will take practice and patience. Don't beat yourself up about it; it is a learning. I learned this doing a lot of work on myself on my own, in counseling, and Partnering With Divinity & Spirit Guides (Chapter 5).

## (7) Am I A Fraud?

Another reason self-trust may get trampled on, is fear of what others think of you or that others might view you as a fraud. But more important is your inner gremlin voice, that may tell you're a fraud, and you might be listening to it. A lot of people experience this. In his series of books, The Power of Positive Thinking, Norman Vincent Peale shares how CEOs, and others with great responsibility, asked him for help because they were in positions of power, and felt they were a fraud. In my coaching practice, there have been several people that felt they were a fraud in their high positions, or a fraud for wanting to create a business. It's that inner gremlin that echoes in one's head, "How can I do that or be that? Am I really equipped?" A gremlin can create a lot of havoc.

## (8) Perfection

Perfection is an illusion. One can always strive to do better and be at one's best, which can move a person forward in wonderful ways. But perfection can create a self-perpetuated ceiling that may be challenging to surpass. The unconscious may create negative side effects when trying to pass beyond that ceiling because one is attached to perfection.

Perfection can also be used as an excuse not to further one's life in some way, because one tells their self they must first have a perfect plan and have everything lined up and completed first. You create your reality. If your outline or plan needs to be perfect, it can be an excuse that blocks you from moving forward, delaying or stopping your progress. You can try outlining what it is you want to achieve, then list ways it is achievable, and list your challenges or obstacles. This can give you a head start on what you think, feel, and want.

## (9) Ego vs. Empowerment

Empaths are frequently challenged with their own power. Many have expressed that when they hear the word "power" they think of something negative, like powerful people that are harmful to others, i.e. "power over" others, rather than power with one's self. And so many empaths give up their power in a culture where growing up with extrasensory gifts and knowing was perhaps unwelcome, and are yet to take back their power. As an adult it may have become a self-limiting process. You may feel you know things but limit yourself to what you are "allowed" to know, feel, hear, or see in your extrasensory skill set. Your gifts, once unlocked and powered up (i.e. activated), can be used to support you and your loved ones.

If we consider that we are living on a soul journey in soul continuance (Chapter 4), as we grow and evolve to access higher consciousness, understanding, and unconditional love, it makes no sense to embrace ego. It's my belief that ego is something a person uses to fight a world they feel at odds with. And in that fight is usually a gremlin again talking you down, causing you to compete against something unseen.

If you gave away your power, then it is something you can get back. It is not a power over anyone else, but instead to be used as a humble power, in love and compassion. A power in being who you are truly meant to be and bringing that to the world if you so choose. Your inner power can propel you forward and motivate you. If you prefer to call it empowerment, then do that.

## (10) Judging

People judge others when they feel they have no control or power over their own life. By judging, I don't mean discernment, which is of great value. Judging others might be an ego play, looking down on others, and is often a habit. Judging casts a shadow over other people and over one's self. It is a view that others are not good enough and don't measure up to what you expect of them, and you are not good enough either. Judging can lead people to gossip, in order to feel better about their self. There is much judging in our culture. It is catabolic and breaks down connections, rather than growing and evolving one's connection with self, others, and the world at large.

\*    \*    \*

So what can be done with all of this?

... **1. Conscious Awareness.**   Seek to become conscious of what is going on in your life, internally. See if you relate to any of the items in this chapter. Identify what is working against you, burdening you, and see if you can process through it. You can start with journaling. Next in partnering with divinity and your spirit guides, you can ask for assistance in understanding, guidance to help with changes you seek, and for help in unburdening you. There are times we can all use extra support, and we must ask for it to receive it. In both journaling and meditation, your higher self will eventually step in and help guide you as well.

... **2. Self-Trust: What Would It Take?**   Ask yourself what it would take for you to trust yourself in what you feel, know, see, and hear? What would need to happen for you to take a leap of faith?  Listen to what comes up for you in the days, weeks and months ahead, and in your meditation.

... **3. Gems Of You.**     See Assignment in the follow-up section at the end of this chapter.

... **4. Gratitude.**     See Assignment in the follow-up section at the end of this chapter.

*     *     *

Writing things can set an intention.  Some say it can alter the brain in creating new pathways.

**Your Inner Compass & Accessing your Intuition**

These days more people seek to learn how to access their intuition and/or access extrasensory information than perhaps fifteen years ago. It is no longer woo woo in our culture.  Business leaders have hired me because they liked my combination of mindfulness (teaching meditation) and being a highly intuitive coach. The skills we have as empaths are becoming more popular now in whatever we do.  You can be proud of who you are.  When you're not shutting yourself down, you are highly gifted in intuition.

**The Body Compass**

As empaths, we are highly aware of our energetic connection to all things.  However, have you considered that your body has knowledge and can also be your compass? When the brain shuts off from remembering, the body still remembers and stores it as cellular memory.  Our body has knowledge of what is best for us, what we are most aligned with or not aligned with, if we listen to it.

Being human receptors (Chapter 1), our DNA is an electrical transmitter-receiver. We are instruments so to speak. When we tap into our instrument as an empath, our extrasensory tuning can guide us in our next right step. This is a major part of our inner compass, our intuition.

After meditating awhile, you might be better able to embrace a mix of things as part of your intuitive tools, one of them being listening to what your body is telling you. When younger, I'd push ahead when my intuition told me not to. The resistance I created regarding what I needed and wanted, would cause me to become ill, repeatedly.

As mentioned in prior chapters, slowing yourself down for a bit each day can allow you to get in touch with so much; one of which is your body compass as an intuition tool.

I worked in the corporate sector for a great many years and loved it. Along the way, personal changes caused me to no longer love that same environment or the work I did there, and yet I pushed forward with it anyway in spite of what I felt. When seeking a new job in the same type of environment and work that I knew so well, though I had great skills and a solid background, I did everything you can imagine to sabotage every interview and would frequently get ill with a fever the night before or the day of the interview. It was my body trying to get me to listen, telling me this is not where you want to be and not what you want to do. I would ask others why I couldn't get a job in the industry I knew. My body knew the answer, but I wasn't listening. Instead, I tried to swim against the tide of who I am and what I wanted. It was unconscious.

Your body compass is one more tool to help you pay attention to what is going on with you, and to awaken your intuition to the knowledge you have access to. Have you ever thought you wanted to pursue something but every time you thought of it, you felt your body react in one of these ways?

- heavy-weighted
- stomach tightened in a knot
- chest constricted
- throat closed
- breath cut short

That is your body telling you, no, or at least for now, no this is not for you. This is your body connecting to your higher self and what it is communicating to you.
Did you ever question pursuing something, whether it was in the work arena, a new idea in your business, or dating a new person, and your friends thought it was a bad idea? Yet every time you thought about it, you felt:

- excited
- motivated
- freeing
- lightness of being
- expansion

That is your body telling you, yes this is a good idea.

I've been aware of my body compass my whole life, tightening in my body and shortened breath versus expansion in my body, feeling lighter, and breathing freely. One makes you feel bad; the other makes you feel good. One's like a closed door; the other door is open with free passage awaiting.

I didn't listen to it when I was younger because I was in conflict with myself. When that inner conflict no longer existed, I was able to listen with close attention to it. You might be interacting with someone regularly on a project or some other thing, and think it is going well, and suddenly your body shuts down about it. And then you find the person you were interacting with is undermining the plans you were making together. Your body knew, before you consciously did. It's part of our empath body compass, our intuition.

So how do you tap into that if your mind is not yet conscious to what your body knows.

## Intuition

Definition of intuition:

> 1. the ability to understand something immediately, without the need for conscious reasoning; and

> 2. a thing that one knows or considers likely from instinctive feeling rather than conscious reasoning.

Some questions to ask yourself:

(1)  Are you open to and allow your intuition?

(2)  Are you slowed down (for 10 minutes a day) enough to connect with your intuition or gut instincts in fleeting moments?

(3)  On a scale of 1-10 (10 being the most), how much do you trust information you receive through intuition, without any way to vet it?

(4) On a scale of 1-10, what is your track record in receiving information you later learned to be correct. Journaling helps you track your progress.

(5) Do you abide by your intuition?

(6) If your intuition is shut down, what do you think is causing it? What is getting in your way?

## Using Body Compass Information

Our body compass works in coordination with our mind, body, and spirit; one affects the other. Our bodies let us know whether we are aligned with what we think and do. And while at times we may be unsure of something, our body knows; it is connected with our intuition. In this intuition our body will expand or contract based on what we're thinking, feeling, and knowing.

To assist in using the body compass tool, I suggest reading the book: Your Inner GPS: Follow Your Internal Guidance To Optimal Health, Happiness, And Satisfaction. I have not read it, but heard an interview of Zen Cryar DeBrucke, one of the authors, on the radio show Coast To Coast AM. She said it is not intuition she is speaking of but rather a process that can be used for guiding one's self. Maybe it is different for an empath being that we are profoundly clairsentient, but I believe this is exactly what is connected to our intuition, our body compass, and that it is part of the mechanism we empaths use to connect to our higher self, divinity, and our spirit guides.

DeBrucke says the information we receive comes to people repeatedly knowing things one can't possibly know. As empaths, we frequently do that without using the body compass, so the body compass (what I call it) would be an extra tool for us. In her radio interview, she offered many examples of how she uses this method, and in more ways than one might imagine. I trust her book has those examples and would be useful for you to read.

Esther Hicks is well-known for channeling a soul group she calls Abraham. She says we all have an installed internal guidance system. I believe this is part of our DNA electrical transmitter-receiver mechanism that we all have as human receptors.

DeBrucke further said in her interview that there is an opening and closing sensation we get that lets us know whether we are in alignment with our self or not. To take this a step further for us empaths, I believe that when we are in alignment with our soul path or soul purpose and what we are meant to do in our life, our higher self works well in conjunction with our body compass.

In addition, DeBrucke said when something is "not true," or "not going to happen," or in my words, is not in alignment with what we need or want, we feel it in contraction or tightening, and our body compass tells us what we need to know. While people in general can learn to do this, as empaths being so deeply connected to energy, including our own, this can be a very powerful thing to tap into. DeBrucke uses this method to forecast various things. For example, you can forecast if it's a good time to have a certain conversation with someone.

NOTE: Something to consider, which can complicate using this tool – several years ago I learned in a Chinese healer class that if a person experiences their throat close, they may be in emotional pain leftover from a love relationship. It can reveal something unresolved, not yet healed. So, if you get a tightening in your throat when trying this body compass intuition tool, first check-in with yourself as to whether you have unresolved emotional pain regarding love, before determining this tool is telling you something else is not good for or you shouldn't move forward with it.

There is an Assignment in the follow-up section at this end of this chapter to try your body compassion intuition. So as not to experience disappointment, keep in mind this Assignment may be more doable for an empath, after processing through the following three items:

... 1. Empath Toolbox. You've adopted tools to live in your own energy, and have other's energies and emotions become peripheral like background noise (Chapter 2).

... 2. Your Empath Gifts. You have identified your empath gifts and better understand your skill set in how you receive information (Chapter 3).

... 3. Self-Doubt. Your self-doubt has decreased and your self-confidence has increased so you can trust more of what you feel (Chapter 3).

After you've gotten more comfortable with the above, listening to your body compass can be much less confusing and very rewarding. The reason accomplishing the above precludes using the body compass intuition tool, is because the contraction method (closing) used here is similar to what occurs with an empath when they absorb negative energy from others (anxiety, fear, stress, worry, overwhelm).

There are a lot of successful people in business and life that use this body compass method without realizing it. They may call it a gut instinct. Such people may listen to what their gut tells them, even if the odds to achieving what they want seem out of range, and repeatedly find it of great value.

An example of how this works is that I sensate in my body immediately when something or someone isn't right for me to move towards or interact with, my whole body immediately tightens. If someone is dishonest, not meaning what they say, or not aligned with what they represent, I feel constriction as though my body shuts down. Empaths are very in tune with others in this way. The next time you feel strongly that someone is being dishonest with you or misrepresenting something, see where in your body you constrict so you can pay attention to how it feels. The next time you are not thoroughly sure, you can check in with your body compass in that part of your body, i.e. in how you react. This tells me when something isn't right or I need to go in another direction. It will usually come to me out of the blue, and prove itself to be true.

In the evening, when quiet and by myself, there may be times when I have thought of someone, my body contracted, I felt uncomfortable, and my breathing was constrained. I then heard in my head that I need to pull back or move away from that person, without yet knowing why. Then days later, or sooner, I learn the reason why. It is always aligned with my body compass and what I need to move away from or go towards.

Sometimes I might have questions about what I'm receiving. I call this static, which is what it feels or sounds like to me, radio static. I usually know where and who it's coming from.

Static for me is usually a sign something is not going well. Meditation activates the crown chakra, allowing for knowing and receiving information in this way.

When I feel contraction, closing, or static about something, it sets me in a different direction at that point, to something that might work better for me. Once I start thinking about the new course I might take, my body immediately relaxes. Then I feel strong again, where I didn't before. The element I sensed was working against me releases and I move forward in a different direction, usually with a different decision than I had made when I felt contraction and static. My breathing gets clear, I get a lot of energy, and I start to get ideas for new things in my life and business. I then move into action on what I want. In time, you will be able to use this tool as to whether something is good for you or not, even when you don't yet know why. I do this in all areas of my life on things that matter most to me. There is much to learn, so learn one thing at a time, and go easy on yourself.

When I started my coaching practice in 2010, I'd never had a business before and had much to learn. I would use my body compass often, asking myself, "If I do this in my business will it help?" By the response I got in my body, I would either move ahead or change direction, and it would often prove to be true. When I did try moving ahead in a direction my body compass said no to, it proved to work against me. I would experience a setback, or a roadblock I could not pass.

Self-trust is crucial in utilizing this tool, but you can use confirmation of what you feel by asking in meditation, partnering with divinity and your spirit guides, and in using tarot cards.

The body compass is just another tool that can be used to help you make decisions aligning with your soul path and life purpose.

_____

## Chapter 9 : Follow-Up Items

(1)  Assignment #1:  Reading A Person Using Your Senses
(2)  Assignment #2:  Gems Of You List
(3)  Assignment #3:  Gratitude List
(4)  Assignment #4:  Exercise: Feel Your Body Compass
(5)  Reference, Book:  Your Inner GPS
(6)  Reference, Book:  The Power of Positive Thinking

_____

(1)  **Assignment 1 : Reading a Person Using Your Senses**

Instructions:
Bring a small pad to jot down your results.  Walk along a street by yourself where there are people, but not a huge crowd.  Look at the ground as you walk.  When you feel someone walking towards you or near you, without looking at them, what do you feel from them?

- Happy
- Sad
- Confused
- Depressed
- Anxious
- Angry
- Calm
- Neutral

Now look up at the person. Do they look as you felt them: Was there a match? Do this with 5 people. How many do you feel you read correctly, just by sensing them?

## (2) **Assignment #2:  Gems of You List**

Write a list of the Gems Of You. Things you like or love about yourself, things that make up part of your greatness, your essence, what makes you ... you, i.e. your gems.

Also contact 3 people you know, and ask them what they like or love about you, and add it to your list. As you go forward add more items to your list.

## (3) **Assignment #3 :  Gratitude List**

Write a list of what you're grateful for.

Write everything small or large, whether individuals in your life, things about yourself, circumstances in your life, what you like to do, items you enjoy, etc. As you go forward. add more items to your list.

On days you feel down or drained, read your Gratitude List and Gems Of You and see if it empowers you.

## (4) **Assignment #4 :  Feel Your Body Compass**

I heard this from Zen Cryar DeBrucke in an interview. See if you can feel what she speaks of in her exercise (what I refer to as your body compass). I recommend reading her book for various examples of how she uses this in daily life.

Instructions:

... 1. Sit in a chair with both feet on the ground, hands in your lap, eyes closed.

... 2. Become aware of the bottom of your feet and how they feel.

... 3. Become aware of how the palms of your hands feel.

... 4. Listen to the sounds around you.

... 5. With the awareness of steps (2-4) above, relax those parts of you, hear this sentence either aloud from someone else or say it aloud yourself:
**"I DO NOT have an Internal Guidance System."**
Say it again.

... 6. Repeat steps (2-4). With the awareness of steps 2-4, relax those parts of you, hear this sentence either aloud from someone else or say it aloud yourself:
**"I DO have an Internal Guidance System."**
Say it again.

Did you feel any difference in your body when you heard each of the above-bolded sentences. I.e. when you heard you didn't have an inner guidance system, did you feel your body tighten in your throat, chest, upper solar plexus, your breathing? When you heard you did have an inner guidance system, did you feel your throat, chest, and upper solar plexus relax? Did your breathing open up?

This shows how our body not only reacts to what we hear, which we feel deeply in our bodies, but also in how our body compass can be a tool for us in knowing things, so we can take action or not in what best serves us. For further insight and examples, see the below reference book.

_____

(6)  Reference, Book:  **Your Inner GPS: Follow Your Internal Guidance To Optimal Health, Happiness, And Satisfaction**, Zen Cryar DeBrucke and Sonia Choquette

_____

(7)  Reference, Book Series:
**The Power Of Positive Thinking**, Norman Vincent Peale

# Chapter 10

## BOUNDARIES

What are boundaries?  Why are they important?

### Definition of Boundaries

1.  Personal Boundaries

    Guidelines, rules, or limits that a person
    creates to identify reasonable, safe, and
    permissible ways for other people to behave
    towards us.

2.  Physical Boundaries

    A physical boundary is a naturally occurring
    barrier between two areas.  Rivers, mountain
    ranges, oceans, and deserts can all serve
    as physical boundaries.  Many times, political
    boundaries between countries or states form
    along physical boundaries.

    - What do boundaries have to do with being reasonable
      or safe?
    - Do you think boundaries offer "permissible ways" for
      people to behave towards us and vice versa?

Though most people don't seem to think much about
boundaries, the reality is people generally treat you how you
teach them to treat you, or don't teach them.  If there are no
guidelines regarding what you need and want, and you do
not teach others where you draw the line, then the line is
blurred.  There may no boundaries.

Most people have no clue they are crossing boundaries or stepping into someone's personal or sacred space. Just like children try to push boundaries with their parents, most adults unconsciously push boundaries. For children, teaching them boundaries helps them to value people, their self, and gives them more understanding of what others need and want from them, so that they know what to bring to the table to interact and feel good about what they offer. It also helps them as they grow up to adopt boundaries they may need for themselves. Without boundaries, children may feel lost and somewhat abandoned. As adults, interacting without boundaries, whether personal or work-related, can create more friction between people than is necessary.

## Empaths & Boundaries

Clairsentience, absorbing energy, emotions, and/or physical symptoms of others, can feel like an invasion of one's being, no different than if someone trespassed and invaded your home. Except the home that is being invaded on a regular basis, is you. Boundaries can be metaphoric walls that protect and house you. If the walls and ceiling were not there, you could be rained on, flooded, and invaded by things that don't belong in your home.

The same thing occurs with people and boundaries. Though boundaries are important for all relationships, for empaths it has added importance with clairsentience, as one may be challenged with "what is me and what is someone else."

## Allowing Boundaries

Though one may be a clairsentient, experiencing merging energy of others with ours, boundaries are hardly ever considered. Instead, many empaths pull back and withdraw from others and may shut down what they feel. This may cause an empath to feel lonely and though some empaths may marry, they may exclude others except for some family.

While withdrawing from others for some can be due to the effects of a challenging childhood yet to be resolved or healed as an adult, it is possible that when empaths learn the Empath Toolbox and have boundaries, they may yearn to be more social. Boundaries need not be punishing or push people away. It is more about educating others on what works for you and what doesn't.

While in the workplace, guidelines are more about what is expected of you, you can still let coworkers know in a kind and maybe humorous way when they cross the line. How else will they know? In one's personal life, friends and family often cross the line in boundaries, with expectations they may have of you. In personal group dynamics, there may be roles each person expects you to play. It's possible that not all of the roles are aligned with who you are in true, authentic self. Learning what your true self needs to feel strong, satisfied, and joyful, will point you to your guidelines, your boundaries. It is a learning.

## Boundaries vs. Stress

Lack of boundaries can be a stress factor in people's lives, empath or not. It can make a person feel triggered, affect self-esteem, and can make a person shut down. When stressed, one might make decisions only to please others, even though the outcome of that decision is not really wanted. People-pleasing is extremely common with empaths, in the hope of avoiding the discomfort of being judged.

Also many empaths feel it is their duty to make everyone else happy, but not their self. Sound familiar? If so, see the Assignment Affirmation in the follow-up section at the end of this chapter. If you spend a lot of energy making everyone else happy and comfortable, are you also making yourself comfortable? Do you experience satisfaction, or do you leave yourself behind, feeling less than. The next time you avoid setting boundaries, in order to make everyone else happy except you, ask yourself: Is everyone else more important than you are?

Boundaries can:

(1) allow for clarity regarding what you feel;

(2) allow others to know you better in what is important to you; and

(3) allow speaking up for yourself, and letting go of worry about being judged.

The fear of being judged is also very common with empaths. It is helpful to become aware of what you are feeling.

**Steps Before Creating Boundaries**

How do you create boundaries, especially in relationships that already exist? It's doable and can be done in less time than one might imagine.

(1) Having absorbed others and felt what others felt instead of what you felt for a long time, it may be confusing to know what you yourself feel. Perhaps give yourself some space and time to allow yourself to feel, think, need, and want whatever comes naturally to you, without censorship. It's possible you might not have considered these things in

yourself before. It may sound simplistic but it's not. See if you can journal about it.

(2) Embrace that you are important, you matter, and that others are not more important than you.

(3) Once you are comfortable with items 1-2 above, you're ready to start standing up and speaking up for yourself, i.e. speaking your truth.

This can be scary, unless you are already empowered. It's new territory and a different approach than people-pleasing, i.e. deferring to everyone else.

To help with this, here is a story of an empath I coached. She always sought to please everyone. She kept her feelings to herself. She rated her stress level at both home and work on a scale of 1-10, to be 10, the highest. She felt everyone took her for granted her whole life. Like most empaths, at no fault of her own, she had no boundaries.

While she was emotionally supportive, loving, and compassionate with her husband of 20 years and their grown children, he was distant and spoke of her unkindly at home, in front of friends, family, and in public. Her grown children did the same, as did her siblings. She said they all bossed her around and treated her like a child.

While she had an amazing background full with degrees, skills, and incredible experience in her industry, at work she was mostly quiet about things that involved her, and was frightened she would be judged and fired. She worked hard, was paid well, and deserved it. Yet she regarded everyone else as more important than she was, at home and at work, and thought what everyone else wanted mattered more than what she wanted. She had no boundaries.

We did role-playing to train her on boundaries and speaking up for herself. At the start, it was terrifying for her and was difficult to allow herself this, as it was something she had never done. In growing up a parent was verbally abusive to her, but not to her siblings. She was the softer of the four siblings, the open and loving one, the empath. In her childhood, she absorbed most of the harshness in the home. The light, love, and compassion she brought to the world was a threat to her abusive mother, a harsh, negative woman who ripped verbally into her daughter tearing her down, and not allowing love and kindness. And there's that word again ALLOW, that affected a young empath in what began her process in life and not allowing herself to feel.

During role-playing she put herself down and made excuses for what she wanted, as though what she wanted required an excuse. The emotional impact of holding back and repressing herself while others pushed her around for so many years, surfaced as anger, pain, and fear. This is quite natural. We worked through the emotions that arose, until she was able to speak of what she wanted without being emotionally triggered. We made action plans for her to respond to the people in her life, and reviewed each response together.

Though at first she sounded conflicted or angry with each person, instead of neutral and open, it still had a profound and positive effect. Her supervisors and coworkers suddenly began to notice her talents rather than her flaws (she had previously felt everyone was looking for her flaws). The boundaries were something they needed in order to see her and get to know her. In 6 months, she was being touted by the organization as a role model employee for all others to follow.  The organization offered her an opportunity to give a speech where politicians might be present.

At home, at the start of speaking up, her anger was abundant; she was unable to contain it. In time, in speaking up and communicating boundaries in what she wanted, she found more balance and she softened.  It had a very positive affect and caused a great change in her marriage, and with her children and siblings.  Her husband began to share more and became kinder and closer with her. Her children showed more affection and appreciation for her.

Why is this?  Everyone in her life needed to know more of what she wanted and how she wanted it.  They all lacked their own boundaries (this is common with people, but it impacts empaths more to their own demise because empaths are loving, wanting to please everyone, and may absorb others' negative emotions).  She had now defined and verbalized to others what was important to her.  Her new boundaries created a structure that others were grateful for.  They could relate more to her, felt closer to her, and it allowed for more satisfying interaction.  They now knew what she wanted and how to provide it.  Her resentment and anger fell away. She had a new found empowerment in communication and felt her empath gifts were no longer a curse, but instead just that, gifts, part of her greatness.  She was able to experience joy more deeply and more often.

**Action Steps To Boundaries**

**(1)  Journal Writing**

Start by journaling what you think, feel, need, and want.  See if you can embrace what emerges without judging it.  Next create a role-playing script, a dialogue between you and someone you need to speak up with. See where it takes you.

## (2) Role-Playing

Find someone who is nonjudgmental that you can role-play with. First have them be the person you need to speak up with. Say what you need, how you need it, and why. If you have anger and frustration, that's natural. After all, you've been holding these things in perhaps your whole life. Journaling can help to release some frustration. Allow it to come out with the friend you are role-playing with. This can help to lessen some emotion, and neutralize it, so when you're ready to speak with the person that you are role-playing about, you can be more focused, without anger. Eliminating anger and emotions in interacting gives you more leverage, impacting what you say. It's referred to as Emotional Intelligence. When removing anger, others may accommodate and appreciate you more.

Then in role-playing with the same person switch roles. Have your friend be you and you be the person you were speaking out with. Continue this until you feel more comfortable with it. By taking on the other person's role, did you learn anything about them or yourself?

Redo the role-playing, as many times as needed, until you feel ready to approach the person in real life. It's okay to be nervous, especially if one is not used to this kind of communication.

## (3) Stand Up & Say It

Now try taking action, by speaking up and setting boundaries with a person in your personal life. Start with one person at a time, until you're more comfortable regarding that person.

Tell them what would work for you, and why. If you need to, tell them what doesn't work for you as well, and why. In this conversation, try not to get into blame, but to explain how something feels for you, i.e. about yourself. Hold steady with what you state you need. Pay attention afterwards to the outcome. Sometimes people are resistant to change and react with habit of what they're used to. That's okay. Try again with that person another time, and give it a second chance.

When ready to speak out at work, this is of course more delicate. Boundaries at work have extra layers requiring understanding guidelines, unspoken rules, hierarchy, showing respect to one's supervisors and elders, while still respecting yourself. It is best to first practice this enough that you are able to let go of triggered emotion, to be neutral.

Boundaries and communication involves a certain amount of understanding. You may delineate and explain what you want and why, and still it might not be understood, and that's okay. The important thing is the attempt, that you have a voice, and that you know you matter, regardless of anyone else's response.

Communication has to do with respecting what someone needs and wants, even if it doesn't make sense. Each person has their own experience they relate to. Allow room for yourself, and also allow room for others. Stand up for yourself, in a kind and unaffected way, stating what you need or want and don't want. It can be communicated in a positive fashion.

## Is Your "Yes" To Someone Else, A "No" To You

Are you challenged in saying no? Been there, done that. Sometimes saying "yes" to something or someone can be like saying "no" to yourself. Remember to take yourself into consideration with every decision you make, no matter how small or large, until you get used to including yourself in the mix, and not leaving yourself behind. At first it may seem like a chore, but in time it will get easier.

Creating boundaries can hold space for one's self in mind, body, and spirit. It creates a platform for growth, defined by you, instead of what was overlaid onto you. Boundaries are one of the crucial steps to putting you in the driver's seat of your metaphoric car and where you want to take it.

---

**Chapter 10 : Follow-Up Items**

(1)  Assignment #1:  Boundaries Quiz
(2)  Assignment #2:  Affirmation: It's None Of My Business
(3)  Reference, Video:  Boundaries, Empathy, and Compassion

---

(1) **Assignment #1:  Boundaries Quiz**
http://www.boundariesbooks.com/boundaries-quiz/
The above assignment is part of a book series, I've not read yet.

**Boundaries**, Dr. Henry Cloud & Dr. John Townsend

## (2) Assignment #2: Affirmation: It's None Of My Business

> It's none of my business,
> what other people think about me.

The above is an old Buddhist saying. It may seem trivial, but using it as an Affirmation altered my life.

The purpose of this Affirmation is:
... (a) to remove pressure and worry of what others think of you, as it can stop your progress;
... (b) a reminder to avoid people-pleasing; and
... (c) to feel good about what you need and want.

Instructions:
Write or say aloud daily, or do both.

... 1. Write it 15 times a day in one sitting. Typing it doesn't work; it's not absorbed.

... 2. If writing is too tedious, you can print and tape it to the back of your cell phone or some place you will see it, and be able to say it aloud repeatedly throughout the day. Or say it aloud before sleep when you are most vulnerable to absorb it.

... 3. It not only sets your intention, but absorbs into your brain, your psyche, until it becomes part of your very being.

... 4. Once you've absorbed it, see if you notice different outcomes.

... 5. Affirmations put us back into alignment with who we really are, taking back our power, and motivating us forward. It rewires and reprograms the brain for a re-set. Some affirmations are absorbed in weeks, some several months. Everyone is different.

_____

(3)  Reference, Video
**Boundaries, Empathy, and Compassion**, Brene Brown
https://www.youtube.com/watch?v=mLTLH3ZK56M

## ABOUT THE AUTHOR

Corri Milner is a Certified Professional Coach (CPC) and Master Practitioner In Energy Leadership (MP-ELI).

In her practice of 3,000 hours coaching since 2010, she has served empaths and others with varied backgrounds, such as: chief executive officers, lawyers, banking executives, military leaders, senior directors, coaches, other business owners, therapists, educators, artists, health facilitators, writers, stay-at-home moms, and everyone in-between.

As an MP-ELI , she offers clients Assessments (done in the privacy of their home), with inspiring readings of it (a snapshot of strengths and possibilities). She also offers Personal Development Programs and Leadership Development Programs. Her programs utilize both coaching and workbooks for those seeking to reduce stress, and to build: self-esteem, emotional intelligence, communication skills, leadership skills, time management, and new outcomes.

She does private 1-on-1 coaching, teaches Healing Meditation with an Energy Reading, Empath Group Programs (5-12 weeks, customized to its members who choose from 29 topics), singular Empath Calls offered only to her Facebook group EMPATHS ON THEIR SOUL PATH, on various empath topics, with presentation and group interaction.

www.corricoaching.com

Services in U.S., international, by phone, online.

Made in the USA
Columbia, SC
26 August 2017